DID I LOVE HIM? YES.
DID I FEEL WANTED? NO.

The situation was this: I did not feel loved at all. Rock was working very hard as his career reached the heights. But whenever he had free moments, he would leave and spend them with his "other" friends. What was my role in his life?

MY HUSBAND, ROCK HUDSON

"What Mrs. Hudson didn't know about her husband filled a book ... She was a farm girl from Minnesota who was ruthlessly manipulated into a marriage that Rock entered only as a public relations maneuver."　　　　　　　　—*New York Daily News*

"A good read!"
　　　　　　　— *Jill Jackson's Hollywood,* McNaught Syndications

"A poignant and believable account ... shocking ... tender and loving."　　　　　— *Daily Journal View Magazine* (Tupelo, MI)

"Gates' Hudson emerges as a complex man who could be romantic one moment, then cold and distant the next."　　— *USA Today*

"I always thought Phyllis was really in love with Rock, and this shows in the book. It's an interesting P.S. to the tormented life of a big movie name whose horrible death ironically brought him everything he had tried to avoid in life."　　　　　— *Liz Smith*

My Husband, ROCK HUDSON

The Real Story of Rock Hudson's
Marriage to Phyllis Gates

PHYLLIS GATES & BOB THOMAS

JOVE BOOKS, NEW YORK

This Jove book contains the complete
text of the original hardcover edition.

MY HUSBAND, ROCK HUDSON

A Jove Book / published by arrangement with
Doubleday, a division of Bantam, Doubleday, Dell Publishing Group, Inc.

PRINTING HISTORY
Doubleday edition published 1987
Jove edition / January 1989

ISBN: 0-515-09840-X

Jove Books are published by The Berkley Publishing Group,
200 Madison Avenue, New York, New York 10016.
The name "JOVE" and the "J" logo
are trademarks belonging to Jove Publications, Inc.

PRINTED IN THE UNITED STATES OF AMERICA

10 9 8 7 6 5 4 3 2 1

Contents

	Prologue	1
1	My Life Before Rock	5
2	"Hi, I'm Rock Hudson"	19
3	Rock: The First Twenty-nine Years	32
4	Fling with a Movie Star	40
5	"Let Me Take Care of You"	53
6	*Giant* and James Dean	60
7	An Engagement, Sort Of	71
8	Wedding in Santa Barbara	79
9	Honeymoon in Jamaica and Manhattan	89
10	Newlyweds	100
11	Movie Star's Wife	113
12	Rock Hudson Close Up	124
13	Clash in Rome	131
14	Africa	141

15	Box-Office King	150
16	*A Farewell to Arms*	161
17	"Please, Honey, Can't You Come Home?"	169
18	Homecoming	178
19	Broken Promises	186
20	Aloha	193
21	Revelation	201
22	The Italian Affair	210
23	Life Without Rock	217
	Epilogue	223

Prologue

ON THE MORNING of July 25, 1985, I was at home in the same house where Rock Hudson and I had spent our married life. (I had sold the house years before, then bought it back in 1984—but that is a story for later on.) The telephone rang, and the caller identified himself as a reporter.

"Army Archerd says in his *Daily Variety* column today that Rock Hudson has AIDS. Did you know about it?"

"No," I replied.

"Do you have any comment about it?"

"If it's true, I feel terribly sorry for Rock."

"Do you expect to be talking to him?"

"No. We haven't spoken in twenty-eight years."

The telephone rang all morning. Reporters asked me such questions as: "Did you separate from Rock because you found out he was gay?" "Is it true the studio forced Rock to marry to quell the rumors he was homosexual?" "What about your million-dollar divorce settlement?"

I tried to keep my temper and tell them politely that I had no comment. Finally I shut off the phone and had a friend respond to those who left their numbers on the answering machine. He told the callers that I was sympathetic concerning Rock's illness but that we had had no contact since our divorce.

At last I was alone with my own thoughts, and the impact of the tragedy struck me. Poor, poor Rock. I had learned enough about AIDS to realize that he probably wouldn't live much longer.

I walked around the house in a kind of stupor, and for the first time since I had returned, my mind started forcing me to remember things.

Over there had been a couch where Rock loved to lie with his head in my lap after a day's work at the studio. That's where the big Christmas tree had stood; I remember Demi trying to knock off ornaments with his paw. And the kitchen—what a mess it had been the night Rock served a feast he had prepared all by himself. The storeroom—now my wine cellar—was where Rock worked late at night on his home movies, coming to bed after I had gone to sleep. It was right there in the bedroom that Rock, in a rage, had locked his hands around my neck and started to squeeze.

Most of all I remembered the day our marriage ended, finally. I had gone to Beverly Hills for a session with my psychologist, Dr. Dubois. For weeks I had been pouring out my frustrations in trying to save my marriage. I had tried everything—love, understanding, argument, anger. Finally Dr. Dubois said to me: "Phyllis, aren't you tired of being a doormat?"

Her words were ringing in my head as I drove home, crying so hard I could hardly see the road. Dr. Dubois had used all her skills to seek a solution to my problems with Rock. She had urged me to convince Rock to undergo psychiatric treatment with Dr. Rankin, but he absolutely refused. Now Dr. Dubois was concerned for me, her patient. Already weakened by hepatitis, I was frightfully nervous and couldn't sleep. The smallest incident could send me into paroxysms of crying.

"Phyllis, aren't you tired of being a doormat?"

When I arrived home at ten-fifteen, Rock was still in bed. The sheet was pulled over his head. I sat down on the edge of the bed and talked to him, gently, not out of anger.

"Rock, I have waited three months for you to start therapy with Dr. Rankin. It seems you don't want to help yourself. You make appointments and break them. You keep telling me you will go, yet you never do. Now you say you won't see him again. If you cared anything about our marriage, you would try. But you have shut it out of your mind, and shut me out too. I see no other choice. We must separate."

When I said "separate," I could feel his body twinge, but he didn't speak.

"I'm leaving the house now, and I will return in three hours. When I come back, I want you gone. At this point, I see no future for us."

I drove away from the house not knowing where to go, what to do. I didn't want to see anyone, because I couldn't control my crying. I drove out Sunset through Beverly Hills and on to Beverly Glen, heading toward Wilshire. I came to Holmby Park and stopped. I sat on a bench, watching the old-timers and their lawn bowling, the young mothers with their toddlers. I felt I was safe there. No one would see me.

After several hours, I drove home. Rock was still in bed, the covers over his head. This time I was angry.

"Get out! Didn't you hear me? We are finished!"

Still he remained silent.

"You don't care about anybody but yourself. You never have. Obviously you're going to stay that way for the rest of your life, childish and foolish. Why don't you want to grow up? Don't you think I deserve better? I want a husband, not someone who uses his home like a hotel room. How long did you think I could take it?"

No response. I was beating my head against a brick wall.

"I'm leaving for another two hours. Please, please, be gone when I return."

When I got back to the house, I found a note saying he had gone to the Beverly Hills Hotel.

I made myself a cup of coffee and sat down. So it was over. And he couldn't even discuss breaking up. We had never really had a heart-to-heart talk in the three years we had been together. Rock had spent most of his life in bed with the covers over his head. Well, now he could do it alone.

1

My Life
Before Rock

THE ALARM BELL woke me out of a deep, dreamless sleep. My whole being rebelled at the intrusion, and I turned off the clock and slipped blissfully back into slumber.

My mother's cheerful voice called for me to rise. How could anyone be cheerful at five-thirty on a Minnesota morning in January?

I didn't want to leave the snug comfort of my downy bed, because I knew what awaited me. My bedroom would be almost as cold as the twenty-degrees-below outside. Our farmhouse had only one oil-fed heater, and it could scarcely reach beyond the living room.

"Phyllis! Get up!"

I leaped out of bed, splashed some near-frozen water on my face, and climbed into my school clothes as fast as possible. It was my job to get the school bus ready for my father's route. That meant going out to the barn, starting the tractor, and pulling the bus to unfreeze it.

When I returned to the kitchen, Mom said, "Goodness, Phyllis, your nose is white."

I looked in the mirror and saw that it was. The end of my nose was nearly frozen, and I thawed it with the palm of my hand.

Breakfast was worth getting up for: toast, oatmeal, eggs, plenty of fresh milk and, best of all, Mom's Swedish pancakes, swimming in maple syrup. Small, thin, tender, they were a delicacy I have never been able to duplicate.

"Time to go, Phyllis," my father said, and we left the warm kitchen for the frigid bus. I wore several layers of wool clothing for protection on the long, long ride. School was only ten miles away, but Dad had to pick up my schoolmates over half the county, bouncing down rutted country roads. Then, of course, some of the kids overslept, and that meant honking the horn and waiting until their mothers sent them chasing out to the road.

Since Dad drove the bus, that meant I was the first passenger on and the last one off. We usually struggled home at five-thirty in the evening, just in time for my farm chores, dinner, homework, and bed.

Our farm was between the small towns of Montevideo and Clarkfield, 130 miles southwest of Minneapolis. Dad was half German and half English, and my mother was pure Norwegian. Like so many Scandinavians, Mom's father had emigrated to the similar climate of Minnesota. I remember Grandpa and Mom talking in Norwegian, and it must have rubbed off on me. People sometimes remark that I have a Norwegian accent.

Dad and Mom married when he was twenty-two and she was seventeen, and every year and a half she gave birth to a baby. They arrived in this order: Verna Florence, Benton Leroy (known to us as Bud), Marvis Ione, Russell Leo, Phyllis Lucille. I arrived on December 7, 1925.

My parents owned six hundred acres, and the nearest neighbor was half a mile away. That meant the Gates children had to amuse themselves, and we did. Sometimes my parents went to the movies with the neighbors, who left their children with us. Harlan was the same age as my brother Bud, and LaVon was my age. Whenever we pipsqueaks got in the way of the older kids' games, we were locked in the cellar. Many times LaVon and I would sit for hours on a pile of winter potatoes watching in terror as the chameleons scurried over the floor.

But, as every member of a large family knows, there are wonderful compensations as well. In the winter, we combined our artistic talents to construct snow castles and snowmen. We went skiing, and skated at the rink on the river in Montevideo. The farm had four horses, and Russ took Mame and I rode Kate on all-day rides.

We had lots of fun and lots of fights; sibling rivalry can intensify when you're in a close family. But even though I was often the brunt of their pranks—Russ once put a garter snake in my hat—I didn't feel victimized. There was a great amount of give-and-take, all leavened by Mom's common sense and good humor.

Summer was a wonderful time on the farm. Dad loved to fish; he was a real outdoors man. On Saturday mornings Mom would pack a lunch and we'd all pile in the Buick and drive to the Chippewa River. Dad supplied poles and bait for all the kids, and we fished on the bank for hours, catching sunfish, which we called crappies, and bullheads, which are also known as catfish. That night Mother would fry them for a delicious dinner.

We never swam in the river because my mother was afraid of it. "Now you stay out of the water," she warned us. "That current will suck you under, and it's so muddy we'd never find you." Only in recent years have I been able to conquer my fear of being in water over my head.

When I was four, my brothers and sisters taught me to read. I became an insatiable reader, consuming everything

I could find—newspapers, magazines, books, the Sears Roebuck catalogue. At five I started my formal education in a grammar school where eight grades were taught in one room by one teacher, Irene Skrukrud. She recognized my eagerness to learn and devoted special attention to me.

On Saturdays, the family drove to Montevideo, which had eight thousand inhabitants but seemed like a metropolis to me. While Mom and Dad did the shopping, the kids paid their dimes at the Hollywood Theater to see the latest western of Gene Autry or Tom Mix. On Sunday all of us attended Our Savior Lutheran Church, where each child was confirmed at fourteen. I went on to teach Sunday school.

My mother was everything that a farm wife and mother should be. She worked long, hard days with never a complaint. She was bright and cheerful and supportive, always urging us children to seek our own individuality. Because of her, the family is still close-knit today. All of my brothers and sisters still live in Minnesota, and every summer without fail I visit them.

My father was a quiet man. I'm sure he was constantly concerned about supporting a family in depressed times when his neighbors were losing their farms in mortgage sales. At night Dad loved for me to comb his hair while he listened to the boxing matches on the radio. "Keep it up, keep it up," he would urge when I complained that my arms were tired. And I did because he seemed so content. My brothers would be studying. My sisters were usually sewing. When I finished combing Dad's hair, I would sew too—usually a project for school.

Dad was supportive of us kids, and he had quite a schedule to comply with as we were always busy running back and forth for basketball and football games, play rehearsals, and choir practice. If our schedules conflicted, he would let one of the older kids drive the school bus. Dad cared very much for his five children, and we discussed things together.

Dad had a phobia about cyclones. Whenever a dark cloud appeared on the horizon, he hollered, "Cyclone coming! Everybody get into the cellar!" It seemed to me that we spent half our lives sitting in that dark cellar—which terrified me—waiting for the cyclone that never came. I can still remember my father's anxiety, his fear that his family would be harmed and that his life's work would be swept away by a brutal whim of nature.

When the cyclone finally did come, we weren't home. The whole family went to Russ's high school graduation, and when we returned, the farm was nearly destroyed. One of the barns was halfway down the pasture. The chicken coop had vanished. Machinery and tools were scattered all over. The damage cost Dad a fortune at a time when he could barely support his family.

My transition from grammar school to junior high was traumatic. I had been a coddled child in a one-teacher school. Now I was plunged into the "big city" school at Clarkfield with sixty students in a class. I was terribly shy at first, but soon I adjusted. I managed to maintain a B-plus average. I became a cheerleader, sang in the choir, and played on the basketball team. I acted in school plays.

Walter Williams was my steady beau through high school. He was the basketball center, six feet three, curly hair and big blue eyes (all my life I have been attracted to tall men). In the summer we went to the drive-in theater, which was really a big screen erected in a cow pasture, or we drove thirty-five miles to Marshall, where we danced to the swing bands at the Blue Moon Ballroom.

By the time of my junior year in high school, I was the only one left at home. My two sisters had married, and my brothers were in the Army. On my sixteenth birthday, I was driving home from Sunday school with my father when we heard a voice on the radio: "We interrupt this program for a special bulletin. The Japanese have attacked Pearl Harbor."

"Phyllis, watch what you're doing!" my father shouted. I

was so shocked that I was driving the car straight into a ditch. Dad grabbed the steering wheel just in time to save us.

The war changed everything in Montevideo and Clarkfield. More and more young men were leaving for the service, and labor for the farms was scarce. To manage his six hundred acres, Dad had only himself, an old German handyman—and me.

Dad could no longer drive the tractor because his hands were increasingly crippled with arthritis. The hired hand couldn't drive at all. That left me, and I spent my entire summer bouncing and jiggling over those dusty fields.

By the end of summer, Dad announced we would have to give up the farm. We moved to Montevideo, where he went to work for the water department. I graduated from Clarkfield High School in June of 1943. Although I had the grades for college, there was no way my parents could send me. Three of my girlfriends and I decided to seek our fortunes in the big city, Minneapolis. When I proposed the idea to Mother, I found surprising acceptance. She even sold one of her war bonds to pay for my bus ticket, but she warned me not to tell Dad.

As I expected, Dad said little about my leaving. I knew he loved me, but he couldn't bring himself to express it. We felt the same unspoken sadness as I waved from the bus that would take me to a brand-new adventure.

MINNEAPOLIS WAS DAZZLING to an eighteen-year-old who had never seen a big city before. The four of us found an apartment with one bedroom and a pull-down bed in the living room, just enough to keep our clothes and sleep in— we spent little time there. No problem finding jobs. The wartime manpower shortage created plenty of opportunities for women.

My first job was as secretary to six engineers at the Minnesota Honeywell company—fortunately I had studied shorthand and typing in high school and was proficient at them. After a year of taking dictation from engineers, I was bored enough to look elsewhere. I found work selling sportswear at the Dayton Company, the biggest department store in Minneapolis.

The job was ideal. I could buy clothes at the employees' discount, so I was able to spruce up my wardrobe and learn for the first time how to wear nice clothes. By facing the public all day, I was able to overcome a portion of the intense shyness that had been part of my baggage from Montevideo. Not incidentally, the Dayton job provided ample opportunity to meet personable young men, salesmen, buyers, and customers.

I was footloose and fancy free, though I hadn't intended it that way. Back home, I had thought I was in love with Dewey Sullivan, a Montevideo boy who had become an army flier. He even gave me his wings before he flew off into the wild blue yonder. But after we exchanged a few love letters, Dewey's family moved and we grew apart.

"Hey, they're having a contest for Miss Dayton," one of my dates told me. "Why don't you try out for it?"

I couldn't imagine winning such a thing. But I gave it a try, and to my surprise, I placed second. That was a big boost for my self-confidence as well as the number of dating possibilities.

Acting on a tip from a salesman, I applied for a position in the cosmetics department, selling Lucien Lelong perfume. The new job afforded commissions, so I was able to pay the rent, buy more clothes, go to movies and shows, send presents to Mom and Dad, and still have money left over. I was in a whirl, dating every night, coming home only to sleep and do my laundry.

One of the fellows I went out with came in the store one morning and told me: "They're interviewing for airline hostesses over at the Radisson Hotel. Why don't you give it a try?"

I had never flown in an airplane, and the idea appealed

to me. I hustled to the Radisson on my lunch hour, inquired at the front desk, and was directed to a meeting room.

"I'm sorry, but we're only interviewing women who have already applied," said the man from Mid-Continent Airlines.

"Oh, but I only heard about it this morning," I said plaintively. "Couldn't I apply now?" Within two weeks I was flying to Kansas City to start training as a stewardess, one of six chosen from one hundred and fifty applicants.

My brother Russ argued against my becoming a stewardess, citing the dangers of flying around the Midwest in all kinds of weather. Mother was also frightened for my safety. Dad was concerned, but quiet as always. The danger didn't worry me.

In Kansas City I was quartered in a dormitory along with the other candidates, and we underwent three weeks of training. We learned the parts of the airplane, how to apply first aid. We were instructed: Don't take drunks on board; Don't sit down; Give a passenger a pillow if he looks sleepy; Don't wake him up if he's sleeping; Calm everyone in bumpy weather. And if the weather gets really bad—fasten seat belts, sit down, and pray.

Mid-Continent Airlines flew DC-3's from the Dakotas to New Orleans. The DC-3 was a sturdy old plane, but it had no pressurization and it could bounce like a tennis ball, especially in the Midwestern summer storms. Landing in Rochester, Minnesota, one night, the plane skidded on the ice, and everything that wasn't fastened down flew all over the cabin. Sometimes I came off one of those flights so woozy that I couldn't find the doorknob with my hand.

As we approached Omaha one day, the plane suddenly zoomed upward. We didn't land in Omaha, nor the next two stops. When we finally touched ground in Kansas City, I went to the cabin and asked the pilot what happened.

"Another goddam plane was coming right toward us at Omaha," he ranted. "So close I had prop wash on the windshield! If those sons of bitches in the control tower can't do a better job, I'm not going to land the plane. *You* take care of the passengers." He stalked off the plane to deliver his protest, leaving me to tell the passengers what happened and try to straighten out their flight plans.

It was hard work, walking up and down the aisle in high heels, delivering twenty-one meals and picking up twenty-one trays. On long night flights, I learned to be a good listener. Passengers poured out their troubles to me, some of the saddest stories you ever heard. Men sometimes punctuated their stories with a hand on my knee. That's when I suddenly remembered my cleanup work in the galley.

The pay was fair, but the hours were great. If I worked ten days, I had the rest of the month off. I could spend time in New Orleans, or I could deadhead—airline lingo for catching a free flight on any airline, depending on seat availability—to Miami to visit my Aunt Lou and Uncle Jake. They lived in a trailer park next to Hialeah race track, and my uncle introduced me to horse racing. We also fished in Biscayne Bay.

I was based in Minneapolis, where I shared an apartment with a couple of other stewardesses. On out-of-town stop-overs, I resisted the invitations of pilots, most of whom were married, to share their beds. My steady date was the copilot of another airline, and we tried to arrange our schedules so we could be in Minneapolis together. We shared a love of golf and played every free day.

After two years with Mid-Continent, I was beginning to tire of the routine. In Minneapolis I had to rise before dawn, sometimes in frigid weather, and arrive at the airport at five-thirty to prepare for a seven-thirty flight. Often at the end of a long flight I could do nothing but fall into bed.

The deciding factor came from the flight surgeon. I had been consulting him for ear problems caused by the unpressurized flights. Finally he told me: "Phyllis, I think you should quit flying. If you continue like this, you may cause permanent damage to your hearing." That was enough to convince me to quit the airline and look for a new adventure.

"LET'S GO TO FLORIDA!" My roommate June Johnson had also tired of flying, and she agreed to my suggestion. We landed in Miami and tried to find jobs as secretaries. No luck. The only work we could find was operating elevators in a big hotel. Later we graduated to cocktail waitresses in a Chinese restaurant.

I loved the sun and the water, and there were plenty of chances for dates. I fell in love with an Air Force captain, and he became my first real affair. We grew very serious about each other—at least I did. I was ready to marry him, but he was concerned about his forthcoming combat duty. I saw him again when I moved to New York, but then he was shipped overseas, and the romance was over.

My move to New York was fairly spontaneous. June decided to return to Minneapolis and marry her old flame, a policeman. When a married couple asked me to visit them in New York, I thought, why not?

The couple, as well as other friends I had made on the airline and in Florida, helped introduce me to New York, which I found both electric and bewildering. I still had some savings from my airline pay, so I could afford to be a tourist for a time. I roomed at the Windsor, a small hotel at Sixth Avenue and Fifty-eighth Street, and planned each day's activities over breakfast in the coffee shop.

One morning I noticed a couple of young men sitting at the counter. One of them had rather long hair and wore a leather jacket, jeans, and boots, a uniform I would expect back home, not in Manhattan. The other had a plaid wool jacket, horn-rimmed glasses, and a scholarly, slightly confused look.

"Hi, come and join us for coffee and a sweet roll," invited the one in the leather jacket.

They seemed boyishly innocent, so I sat with them. "I'm Marlon and this is Wally and what's your name?" asked Number 1.

It turned out they hadn't been in New York very long, and they still had enthusiasm for the city. "Today we're going to show you *our* New York," Marlon announced.

The three of us set out in the crisp autumn morning, and we walked for miles through the crowded streets, Marlon and Wally pointing at the landmarks.

By noon we were exhausted, and Marlon steered us to the Russian Tea Room. They were amused as I tried to make sense of the huge menu, and Wally ordered chicken Kiev for me.

"Why don't you come up to my apartment?" Marlon said when we finished lunch. "It's just around the corner. There's someone I'd like you to meet."

Oh-oh, I thought, here it comes. But when we went to his apartment, he only wanted to introduce me to Russell, his pet raccoon. "Let's go to the movies," Wally suggested, and we did. We had lunch on another day, and Marlon called me to ask, "Do you want to go for a ride on a ferry?" I was busy that day, and he didn't call again.

When I told a friend about my adventures, she said, "Don't you know who they are? Wally Cox is a new comedian, and Marlon Brando is a movie star. He was sensational in *A Streetcar Named Desire.*"

A friend invited me to a lavish cocktail party on Central Park West, and then he never appeared. I struck up a conversation with another guest who seemed as lost as I was. His name was Ray Stricklyn, and he had just arrived from Texas to make a career for himself as an actor. Meanwhile he worked as a secretary at the big talent agency, MCA.

Ray and I became immediate friends, and we often met over coffee in the morning. He told me of a job opening as secretary to an agent across the hall from him: "If you can type and answer the phone, I think I can get you the job."

I became secretary to Maynard Morris, and I soon realized why my predecessor quit. He was a fussy, high-strung man who wanted things done immediately. He spoke in half sentences because he was too impatient to get the words out. My biggest problem was learning who was important and who wasn't, since the world of show business was totally foreign to me. Fortunately Ray was seated nearby.

"Psst, Ray," I whispered. "Somebody named Darryl Zanuck is on the phone. Should I put him through to Mr. Morris?"

I began dating a lawyer who delighted in introducing me to the wonders of New York—the concerts, galleries, plays, and nightclubs. One night he took me to a club that featured the hottest cabaret act, Kay Thompson and four energetic young singers, the Williams Brothers. I was surprised one morning to find myself having breakfast in the hotel coffee shop next to one of the brothers, Andy. He struck up a conversation, and I told him how much I had enjoyed his show.

"Hey, I'm making a record tonight, just myself without the brothers," Andy said. "Would you like to watch?"

"Sure," I said. He picked me up at the hotel that night and we drove to the recording studio. Over dinner in a small café, Andy spoke eagerly of his plans to leave Kay Thompson and his brothers and seek his own career. His enthusiasm was endearing, but at the hotel elevator I declined his offer to accompany me upstairs. That was the last I heard from Andy.

I loved New York, but I hated my job. As soon as Maynard Morris entered the office, my stomach started to churn. I quit MCA and found another secretarial job with American National Theater and Academy. The work was much more pleasant, and I felt I was becoming a confirmed New Yorker. Then came the day in Greenwich Village that changed my life—and almost ended it. It was Friday, the thirteenth of March, 1953.

I STOOD ON A STREET CORNER lost in thought. As soon as the traffic signal turned red, I stepped off the curb. I guess I hadn't been in New York long enough to realize that a pedestrian had to make sure that drivers were observing the signal too. All I remember is the screech of tires on pavement and myself becoming airborne. Then a crowd of people staring down at the pitiful figure. An ambulance shrilling through the Manhattan streets. Doctors gravely assessing the damage to a human body.

I woke up in the emergency hospital and was unable to move. My left leg had been broken in four places, my pelvis had two breaks. I had a concussion and internal bleeding. Some of the skin of my face had been scraped away by the pavement.

On Monday I was moved to the Hospital for General Surgery, where doctors tried to put my leg back together. They screwed the bone pieces to a steel plate, then sewed me back up. I carried that plate until eighteen years ago, when it was removed.

After four months, I hobbled out of the hospital on crutches, my leg still in a cast. I recuperated in my hotel room, having meals sent up from the dining room. The hospital nurses had become good friends, and they often visited me, later taking me to movies on their days off. Fortunately I had no money worries. The insurance company of the driver who struck me conceded his guilt—one of my witnesses was a state supreme court judge! All of my hospital and medical expenses were paid, and I received a $10,000 settlement.

Through one of the doctors in the hospital I had met Steve Evans, and we immediately became friends. He was an affable young man who worked in the restaurant business in Los Angeles. He cheered me up with amusing stories about actors and other characters he knew. One day he suggested that I go to California.

"You would adore it," he said. "You'd recover fast in the sunshine, and I know you'd make a hit, you're so cheerful and friendly. My girlfriend is giving a party for New Year's. Why don't you come out for it?"

His prescription seemed like just what I needed. I packed my belongings, said good-bye to all my New York friends, and departed for Christmas in Montevideo, where I graduated from crutches to a cane. Then off to California!

I arrived on December 28, 1953. Flush with my insurance settlement, I registered at the Beverly Hills Hotel. For a whole week I lived in a splendor I had never known before. By the end of that time I realized that this was where I wanted to spend the rest of my life. I celebrated my decision by buying a red Ford convertible.

2

"Hi, I'm Rock Hudson"

"OKAY, PHYLLIS, you've been goofing off long enough,"
said Steve Evans. "It's time you found an honest job."

He was right. For almost six months I had been savoring
the California life. I spent hours on the Santa Monica sands,
trading my eastern pallor for California bronze. I walked
along the beaches and in the hills to strengthen my leg, and
I played golf at Rancho Park. I made dozens of new friends,
and I blissfully adjusted to the relaxed lifestyle after the
staccato of New York.

"Do you have any suggestions?" I asked Steve.

"As a matter of fact, I do," he replied. "Yesterday I heard
about an agent who needs a secretary. You worked for an
agency in New York, didn't you?"

"Sure—MCA."

"Then I'll arrange for you to meet him. He's kind of a

strange character, but he's damned successful. He's the guy who named Rory Calhoun, Tab Hunter, and Rock Hudson. His name is Henry Willson."

Steve arranged for us to meet at Scandia, a successful restaurant on the Sunset Strip just a block away from where I was staying in a small hotel. I joined Steve late one afternoon in the Scandia bar, which was dark and leathery and decorated with steins, horned helmets, and other macho gear.

"Henry will be late, he's always late," Steve said after we ordered drinks and the large meatballs that were the house specialty.

"Telephone call for Henry Willson."

Patrons in the bar turned their heads in automatic response to the announcement on the loudspeaker. Whoever Henry Willson was, I concluded, he must be important.

Twenty minutes later, Henry Willson appeared at our table. He was breathless. Instead of responding to Steve's introduction, he said: "I shouldn't hire you as a secretary. I should get you a studio contract."

He sat down, ordered a whiskey and soda. Before I could speak, a voice announced: "Telephone call for Henry Willson." He rose immediately and disappeared into the lobby. When he returned, he explained: "That was New York. They want Natalie Wood on 'The Ed Sullivan Show' next Sunday. I'll let her do it, but I want them to sweat for a day."

Henry again took his seat, and he started talking. He explained that he had been talent scout for David O. Selznick for six years, discovering Guy Madison, Rhonda Fleming, and others. When Selznick ran into financial troubles, Henry joined a large talent agency. "But what the hell, they were just capitalizing on my discoveries," he said. "So I started my own office."

He continued talking nonstop, affording me the chance to study him. Although he wore an expensive black silk suit with an immaculate white shirt, beautiful tie, and matching handkerchief in his breast pocket, his exquisite grooming could not compensate for his basic unattractiveness. His face was a misshapen mask: the weak chin, the fleshy lips, the bulbous nose, the wide-apart lifeless eyes, heavy eyebrows, and receding black hair. You could understand why he made a career of discovering and exploiting beauty.

"What I need, Phyllis," he continued, "is someone with taste and discrimination and tact. With all the publicity I've received about discovering and naming stars, every kid in the world is banging on my door. Most of them are pathetic, and I don't want to waste my time with them. But I also don't want to miss another Rock or Tab. You can weed them out for me, can't you, Phyllis?"

"I think so, Mr. Willson," I said hesitantly.

"Please—it's Henry. I know you can." He glanced at his watch. "Shit! I've got a date at Columbia with Harry Cohn. You take her over to look at the office, will you, Steve? That's a good lad. Phyllis, nice to meet you. Come to work, nine o'clock Monday. See ya." He vanished.

"Whew, that was quick," I said to Steve.

"That's Henry. Always in a hurry, always making snap decisions. Usually he's right, about talent, anyway. He's an absolute genius at finding and packaging personalities."

ON MONDAY MORNING I put on my best skirt and blouse and drove to 1046½ Carol Drive, a few steps from Sunset Boulevard at the end of the Strip. I walked up the steps and entered a large room with two desks. A pretty young woman sat behind one of them.

"Hi, I'm Pat Devlin," she said. "Are you Henry's new secretary?"

"Yes, I'm Phyllis Gates. Nice to meet you."

"Thank God you're here. Henry has been driving me nuts. 'Do this!' 'Do that!' You'd think I worked for him."

Pat didn't work for Henry Willson. Her boss was Ben

Pearson, an agent who rented the upper floor of the building and sublet half to Henry. The lower floor was occupied by Four Star Productions, the television operation of Dick Powell, Charles Boyer, and David Niven.

"That's your desk," Pat Devlin said. "Henry's office is behind you. The ladies' room is down the hall."

Her phone started ringing, so I placed my purse in the drawer of my desk and walked into Henry's office to see if I could learn more about my new boss. The office looked surprisingly spacious, considering how small the building seemed from the outside. The furnishings were done in high style: a long, modern desk; two chairs opposite, covered with a Tahitian cotton fabric; a low couch at the opposite end of the office; a chrome and glass bar in the corner. Along two walls were photographs of Hollywood figures such as Ingrid Bergman, Lana Turner, David O. Selznick, Joseph Cotten, Shirley Temple, Jennifer Jones. Each was autographed with an inscription like "To Henry, with deepest thanks for your help" or "You are the best agent I know."

The wall behind Henry's desk was reserved for his clients, and here the inscriptions were more effusive: "To Henry, where would I be without you?" and "God love you, Henry." Among the young and beautiful faces were Natalie Wood, Sheree North, Rory Calhoun, Tab Hunter, and Rock Hudson. I paused for a moment at the portrait of Rock Hudson. I had seen him on the screen only once, with Jane Wyman in *Magnificent Obsession*, a movie that made me weep like a schoolgirl. As I studied his almost-perfect face, with a crinkle at the eyes denoting he was not stuck-up about it, I could understand why he was such a favorite with teenage girls.

Henry Willson breezed into the office about ten-thirty. I soon discovered that was his normal manner. He seemed forever on the move, hurrying into the office and then dashing off for lunch in a studio commissary or drinks at the Cock 'n Bull, an English pub and restaurant a few doors from the office. He accomplished his work over cocktails and studio lunches and in executive suites. The necessary office duty bored him. When I typed letters for him to sign, he always scrawled, "Hastily, Henry."

Henry hated to drive and he disliked the trivial routine of normal living. So he enlisted a small legion of helpers: his young and eager clients. They became his slaves, driving him to appointments, picking up his laundry, shopping for his groceries. Whenever one of them protested, Henry had a ready answer: "You want to get a contract, don't you? You want to be a star, don't you?"

Even with my Midwestern naïveté, I soon discovered there was something different about Henry. There was nothing effeminate in his dress or manner, but he was not exactly what you would consider manly. He adored gossip, preferably of the nasty kind, and he could be bitchy about people he didn't like. If he had a fight with one of his clients, Henry would call him "that queer."

In a lighter moment, Henry would stand up in his office and perform bumps and grinds with the skill of a burlesque stripper. He did it for an audience of one—me—and I was convulsed. "You know I started out as a dancer," he remarked. "Took lessons and everything. But I decided I'd be better off discovering people who had more talent than I did."

Henry was in his early forties when I went to work for him. I could find out very little about his early life, then or now. Only that he was born in Lansdowne, Pennsylvania, and grew up in Larchmont, New York. Apparently his father was wealthy. Ben Pearson told me that the elder Willson had been president of Columbia Records and had pioneered putting recordings on both sides of a platter. I never found out how Henry got into show business. He first came into prominence as talent head for David O. Selznick at a time when the producer was developing an important stable of stars. Becoming an agent was a natural progression for Henry, and his uncanny sense of what makes a film personality helped fill Hollywood's need for new faces to replace the aging, prewar stars. Most of Henry's clients were in their twenties, but he did represent a few mature personalities, including Jeanette MacDonald and Ann Sothern.

Henry was a chameleon. He could be like a stern father to his young clients. He could be crisp and businesslike with studio bosses. He had a finely honed sense of humor, and he could charm a roomful of celebrities. He could play whatever role was needed to swing a deal or ingratiate himself.

Henry spent hundreds of dollars on clothes for his new clients so they would make a good impression on interviews. He hosted producers and clients at the most expensive restaurants in Los Angeles and never allowed anyone else to pick up the tab. He remembered anniversaries and birthdays with flowers and presents. He was personally immaculate and seemed to have a fetish about washing his hands.

"You wanna meet Margaret Truman?" he asked me one day.

"Margaret Truman?"

"Sure. She's a pal of mine. In town for a concert at the Hollywood Bowl. I'm having drinks with her at the Polo Lounge. Come along."

I sat in awe as Henry and President Truman's daughter spent a hilarious hour talking about her singing career and other matters. Henry began taking me along for other meetings over drinks at the Cock 'n Bull or Scandia or lunch at the studios. He started introducing me as "my assistant."

One morning Henry announced: "I'm going to Hawaii. I feel so comfortable with you minding the store that I'm taking a vacation. You're the most responsible help I've ever had."

I felt complimented and proud. During Henry's absence, I not only managed the office, I also found work for some of the clients. Robert Van Orden was an actor Henry had renamed John Smith to prove that he could also build a star with such a common name. While John wasn't as successful as Rock and Tab and Rory, he did achieve some prominence. I was able to negotiate a lucrative Budweiser beer commercial for him, knowing that television commercials could be a good source of income for clients between acting jobs.

When Henry returned from Hawaii, he was pleased with how I had managed the office. "I should go away on vacation more often," he said.

Henry began giving me more responsibilities. I drove his young clients to interviews at the studios—at my own expense, of course. Henry was paying me fifty dollars a week, with no allowance for mileage. At that rate, I would be broke before the year was out.

A peculiar thing happened at 20th Century-Fox. I escorted a young client for an interview, and I found the casting director staring at me. Finally he said, *"You're* the one I should be interviewing. How would you like to take a screen test?"

"Me? Are you kidding?" I was both amused and terrified. The thought of appearing before a camera gave me the chills. There was absolutely no way I could ever consider becoming an actress. No way! I thanked the man for his compliment and went back to being a junior agent.

Henry was well aware of the value of publicity for his clients—and himself. Often he would tell me, "Get Hedda on the phone," or, "Call Louella." He would impart some tidbit about a client's romance or future film role. He didn't mind at all when the columnist printed: "Henry Willson tells me that Natalie Wood has been cast in *Rebel Without a Cause . . .*"

The Henry Willson phenomenon attracted magazine articles. A *Parade* magazine article by Lloyd Shearer was titled "He Made Rock Hudson a Star." It began with an alleged letter: "Dear Mr. Willson, My name is Ken Yashita.

I am the Japanese Clark Gable. I am 5'2" and have big ears. I also act swell. I want you to represent me for motion pictures. Write me at once."

The article claimed that every year Henry received five thousand letters and sixteen thousand telephone calls from aspiring actors and actresses. The story continued: " 'I'm what you might call a Salvation Army worker at heart,' Willson wearily admits, 'and the kids in this business know it. I earn anywhere from fifty thousand to seventy-five thousand a year, but I don't have a buck to show for it. Why? Because I'm spending it all on the youngsters.' "

Exaggerations, of course, but with an element of truth. Henry indeed spent money freely, many times on behalf of his clients. He also owned a lavish home on Stone Canyon in Bel Air, where he liked to give big parties to show off his discoveries and ingratiate himself with Hollywood's elite.

The onslaught of hopefuls wasn't as great as *Parade* reported, but it was considerable. I spent a large part of my day opening mail with eight-by-ten glossies of pretty young men and women, also answering their telephone calls or talking to those who visited the office. They used every kind of ruse to attract Henry's attention—parading like pickets in front of the building; appearing in bikinis, male or female. One enterprising young man used a fire ladder to reach Henry's office window from the parking lot behind the building, the equivalent of three stories. Henry looked out the window and saw a face peering at him. He was terrified and told me to call the police.

One of the office hazards was the persistently waiting hopeful. A young man would insist that he would remain at the office until Mr. Willson appeared. When Henry finally did arrive, he rushed into his office before he could be buttonholed. He called me in to order, "Get rid of that creep." My efforts usually failed, and Henry rushed out of the office before the hapless young man could present his case.

Among the chronic waiters was a towering young man

with a shy drawl. Henry had spied him as a deputy sheriff at the Sands Hotel in Las Vegas and had given him the familiar line, "If you're ever interested in an acting career, look me up." The deputy did so, but Henry couldn't find the time for him. The office waiting room was pretty small, and finally Ben Pearson complained, "For God's sake, Henry, can't you do something for that giant outside your office?"

"Sure, Ben," Henry said. "I'll take him out to Warner Brothers. They're looking for television cowpokes." He succeeded in selling Clint Walker as the star of "Cheyenne."

Henry and Ben were a contrast as agents. Ben was steady and thorough, an easy boss for Pat Devlin. Henry was flamboyant and unpredictable, and he kept me wondering what he would do next. Ben was a family man who quit at five o'clock and went home to his wife and children. At five o'clock, Henry was just beginning to roll. Sometimes he would entertain his clients and friends in Ben's office, which had more comfortable furniture and a well-stocked bar. (Henry always replenished the supplies.)

Ben, who specialized in nightclub and legitimate theater bookings, had a client list that included such veterans as Joe E. Brown, Judy Canova, Buster Keaton, and Reginald Gardiner. "I don't understand," Henry told Ben, "how a man as intelligent and knowledgeable as you can waste his time on such terribly old people!"

"Listen, Henry," Ben replied, "my 'old people' can earn two hundred thousand a year from doing radio, theater, commercials, and, yes, supermarket openings. How much do your pretty-boys make?"

One day Rudy Vallee came to the office to confer with Ben about a tour in summer stock. At the same time Henry was meeting with a new client, Johnnie Ray, who was then the singing rage with "Cry" and other hit records. The two singers were introduced, and it was a fascinating contrast—Rudy Vallee, the first of the pop singers, and Johnnie Ray, the newest sensation.

"Johnnie has just signed for an Irving Berlin musical with Marilyn Monroe and Ethel Merman," Henry bragged. "He's going to be a big hit in pictures." Wrong again, Henry.

Sheree North called the office one day and said, "I've got an interview with Joe Hyams of the New York *Herald Tribune,* and I don't want to do it at the studio. Is it okay if I do it there?"

"I'm sure it would be all right with Mr. Willson," I replied.

Sheree, who was second in line to Marilyn Monroe as the blonde bombshell at Fox, arrived at two o'clock with Hyams, a tall, good-looking, dark-eyed reporter. Since Henry was using his office, I let them conduct the interview at my desk while I sat in a corner reading magazines.

I soon discovered it was something more than an interview. Sheree and Joe talked intimately, then held hands. They started kissing, and I struggled to keep my eyes on the magazine. After they had necked for several minutes, I finally said, "Look, folks, I've got to get back to work. I need my desk." They departed blissfully, hand in hand.

I BEGAN TO SEE a pattern in Henry's dealings with the young male hopefuls. When he found a young man who was remarkably handsome though not visibly talented, Henry filled him with dreams of stardom. Henry made furtive attempts for studio auditions, but when no interest was expressed, the young man became Henry's gofer, then was discarded.

After eight months on the job, I asked Henry if I could have a vacation. He was indignant at first, claiming I hadn't worked for him long enough. But when I said I wanted to go back to Minnesota to visit my folks, he grumbled, "Oh, all right, go ahead."

Two days later he came rushing into the office and told me, "I've got a suggestion. Instead of spending money on an airline ticket, why don't you ride to the Midwest with a client of mine? He's going back there to visit his relatives too."

"But who is he?" I asked. "I can't drive across the country with a strange man."

"You have nothing to worry about. He'll be a perfect gentleman, I guarantee. And he's got a swell new convertible. I'll invite him to lunch so you can meet him."

A man whom I'll call Bill McGiver came to the office at noon. He was a good-looking blond, medium height, well-dressed, pleasant personality. He was trying to be an actor, but he didn't have enough ambition or vanity. Henry took us to lunch and kept the conversation sparkling in his best manner. Somewhat warily, I agreed to the journey.

Henry was right: Bill was the perfect gentleman. Fun, too. He kept me amused with stories about his folks back home, or else we just listened to the radio. He drove fast and long, so that we made the trip to Minnesota in three days.

He dropped me off at my parents' house, then went on to his relatives, who lived one hundred and fifty miles away. I had a wonderful week with Mom and Dad and my brothers and sisters and their families. Then Bill came for me, and we started on the long trip back to California.

We were driving through Colorado when Bill said casually, "By the way, did you know this is Rock Hudson's car?"

I was surprised. "No, I didn't," I said.

"Yeah, we share a house together. Rock's out of the country, making a movie. Whenever he's gone, he lets me use his car."

"Oh?" I learned later that Rock didn't own the Lincoln. It was loaned to him by the Ford Motor Company, which valued the publicity of having a movie star drive one of its luxury models. Even so, I thought it strange that Rock would entrust the car to his housemate to use any way he wanted, including a cross-country trip.

Bill returned me to my apartment, and I thanked him for

being such a delightful and courteous companion. Shortly afterward his name was dropped from Henry's client list. I never saw him again. I was puzzled by his sudden disappearance. During our trip together Bill had talked excitedly about his dreams of a career in films, and I believed he had the looks and personality to become an actor. But he dropped out of sight. No forwarding address, nothing. I tried to find out something from Henry, but Henry simply made one of the cutting remarks he reserved for ex-clients, and dismissed the matter.

ALTHOUGH I'D WORKED for months at the Henry Willson Agency, I'd never met the most important client. Rock Hudson was in Ireland filming *Captain Lightfoot,* yet his presence was almost palpable. Henry was always talking about him: "Turn down that request—it wouldn't be good for Rock's image"; "The boy has an interesting face, but he's no Rock Hudson"; etc.

Rock Hudson seemed like an obsession for Henry. "I made him a star," Henry proclaimed, and no one could dispute that.

The story of Rock's discovery had been told over and over again in the fan magazine articles that I dutifully clipped for Henry. The more fanciful version claimed that Rock had been a relief mailman who was spotted when he made a delivery to Henry's office.

More likely is the story that Rock himself told in interviews. How he used his earnings from driving a truck to buy a forty-dollar gabardine suit so he could apply for acting jobs. How he sent his photo and description to all the studios and got only one response—from Henry Willson at Selznick. How Henry changed his name from Roy Fitzgerald to Rock Hudson and peddled him unsuccessfully to MGM, Fox, and other studios. How the director Raoul Walsh finally cast Rock in a small role in *Fighter Squadron,* then sold Rock's contract to Universal.

One morning in October, I was busily typing a letter when I sensed that someone had appeared before my desk. I finished typing the sentence, then I turned and looked up. And up. And up.

Towering above me was that familiar face wearing that million-dollar grin.

"Hi. I'm Rock Hudson," he announced needlessly.

3

Rock: The First Twenty-nine Years

OFTEN DURING OUR COURTSHIP and marriage I asked Rock to tell me about his childhood. He always responded with that winning laugh of his and an offhanded remark. That, I was to learn, was his method of ridding himself of unpleasant topics. When I discovered more about his childhood—from other sources, never from him —I realized why he was so reluctant to talk of his early years. We both had Midwestern childhoods, but mine was full of joy and love; his was miserable.

He was born November 17, 1925, in Winnetka, Illinois, and named Roy Scherer, Jr. His weight at birth gave no indication of his future size—five and a half pounds at twenty-seven inches in length. His father, Roy, Sr., operated a garage and was of German and Swiss descent. His mother, Kay, was Irish-English.

Rock's mother told me that he cried for the first three months of his life until she and her mother found a formula that he would drink. When he was six months old, his mother fell while carrying him, and his leg was broken. Otherwise the first four years of Roy's life appear to have been happy ones. The Scherers lived near Lake Michigan, and Kay often took her son to the shoreline where he played on the beach with other children. His favorite times came when he visited his grandparents' farm at Olney, Illinois.

The older Scherers had six hundred acres of farmland, much like the farm of my childhood. Roy loved to follow his grandmother as she milked the cows and fed the chickens. His grandfather perched the boy on the horse as he did the plowing. The Scherers were a warm, simple, close-knit family; nine children had grown up on the farm. Young Roy stayed the whole summer with his grandparents, and he always had visiting cousins to play with.

Roy was six when his world fell apart. The Depression had paralyzed the Midwest, and his father's business had gone bankrupt. Scherer spent his last money to buy a train ticket to California, where he hoped to make a new start. Kay Scherer and her son moved in with her parents, and the house had already absorbed her brother, his wife, and four children. It was a tough period for young Roy, who couldn't understand why his father had left him. His mother and grandmother were constantly bickering.

"Don't give Junior coffee," Kay declared.

"Coffee never hurt anybody," said her mother, pouring a cup.

Kay took Roy to California when the boy was seven. She was confident that she could persuade her husband to return to Winnetka. But Scherer, who was working as a doughnut salesman, had no intention of going back to the place where he had failed. Kay and Roy made the sad journey back to Illinois.

On the bus ride home, Kay met a young marine who was

on his way to honor-guard duty at the Chicago World's Fair. He was a tall, gangly redhead who didn't smoke or drink and had done amateur boxing. Kay was intrigued with Wallace Fitzgerald and joined the card game he was playing with another marine. Kay invited Fitzgerald to her mother's house for Thanksgiving.

They were married in February of 1934, and two months later his Marine hitch ended. Fitzgerald could only find work as a gardener, handyman, or truck driver. Kay augmented their income as a waitress, then she was hired by the telephone company. The Fitzgeralds were able to move from her parents' house to a small apartment.

Rock never concealed his hatred for his stepfather.

"As soon as they were married, all my toys were taken away from me," he once told an interviewer. "My name was changed to his—I became Roy Fitzgerald. I stayed away from home as much as possible for those nine years, and when I was home, I tried to ignore everything."

Even Kay later admitted of her second husband: "He was mean to the boy, and Rock hated him."

Such a situation drew the boy closer to his mother. As Rock once commented, "She was mother, father, and big sister to me, and I was son and brother to her. Regardless of who she was married to, we always had a great affection for one another."

Kay told me that Rock was thin and sickly as a boy, and unhappy at school. By the age of ten he had to work to help the family's finances. He delivered groceries and cleaned chickens for a butcher. A company hired him to take down people's awnings for the winter, but he forgot to label them. In the spring no one could find the right awnings, and Roy was fired. At one time he was delivering for five Chicago newspapers, but there were so many complaints about non-deliveries that he was discharged.

One day in 1938, Roy answered a knock at the door and saw a graying, heavyset man standing before him. "Hi, kid, how are you?" the man said.

"Fine," the boy replied.

Before the man could say more, Roy's mother shouted, "Roy, get away from the door!" He obeyed, and not until later did he learn that the caller had been his own father. Fitzgerald sent a letter to Scherer ordering him "not to write to my son Roy or try to see him again." Roy was twelve, and he wouldn't see his real father again until he was an adult.

As a suburb of Chicago, Winnetka was a mixture of the very rich and the very poor. In his teens Roy was able to see how the wealthy lived. He was enrolled in dancing school —free. The reason was that Roy was a head taller than the other boys, and he made an ideal partner for the girls. He was able to compare his own awkwardness with the smooth manner of the other dancers.

Roy became friendly with Eddie Jenner, whose family owned a five-bedroom home with swimming pool and a staff of five. When Roy was invited to dinner at the Jenner house, he had his first taste of luxury living. He was faced with a bewildering array of silverware. A maid served the dishes, and Roy turned scarlet when he accidentally knocked the serving spoon out of her hand. None of the family remarked on the incident.

Rock always claimed in interviews that his ambition to be an actor began when he saw the movie *The Hurricane.* "It was in 1937, when I was twelve years old," he said. "There was one shot where Jon Hall dived off the mast of a ship and swam across a lagoon to Dorothy Lamour. From then on, I wanted to grow up and be like Jon Hall." (Years later when he was an actor, Rock learned that the dive had been done by a stunt man.)

Kay's second marriage wasn't going well. She and Fitzgerald argued constantly. To help their finances, she suggested buying a big, empty house on Ash Street and taking in boarders. He objected, but Kay was a forceful woman. Fitzgerald complained about all the work he had to do for the house and the trouble the boarders made. When the arguments became overheated, Roy was shipped off to an aunt's house. When he returned, the situation had calmed down.

But in July 1941, when Roy returned from his aunt's, Wally Fitzgerald wasn't there. He had packed his belongings and left the house for good.

Roy was relieved to be rid of the stepfather he detested, but now his mother had little time for him. To support herself and Roy, she had started work as a switchboard operator at the Great Lakes Training Station seventeen miles away. He was asleep when she left for work, and she usually returned after he had gone to bed. After school Roy worked at odd jobs, but he could never keep one for long.

He was supposed to graduate from New Trier High School in June 1943, but he had to stay over to make up some courses. He graduated the following January and enlisted in the Navy a month later.

Roy went to boot camp close to home—the Great Lakes Naval Training Center where his mother worked. He was trained to repair airplanes, then shipped to California and on to Samar in the Philippines. Apparently he was not a very good sailor. He was reprimanded for missing a watch. Once he was warming up a B-26, and he forgot instructions and turned on both engines at once. The bomber leaped forward and smashed into a Piper Cub. Roy was chewed out and placed on mess duty.

In May 1946, Roy arrived back in California for his discharge. Kay was waiting for him on the dock, ready to take him back to Winnetka. Roy was restless at home. Most of his old buddies had left town or were getting married. He worked for a moving company but quit after two weeks. He collected unemployment insurance until the checks ran out, then delivered mail. What he really wanted to do was to be an actor, but he didn't dare tell his mother. "Mom would have told me to get the idea out of my head," he said later.

Roy decided to pursue his secret ambition in California,

where the action was. He wrote to his father, who operated an appliance store in south Los Angeles. Roy Scherer agreed to provide housing for his son, and Roy left for California with two hundred dollars in his wallet. He intended to enroll at the University of Southern California (as I did years later), but his high school grades were too poor. He tried to work as a salesman in his father's store, but he was too tongue-tied to talk with customers. Roy Scherer found him a job driving trucks for a dried-fruit company.

Roy Scherer had no more sympathy for Roy's acting ambitions than Kay Fitzgerald. "Don't mention actors to me," Scherer snapped. "They're unreliable and they're unstable."

But Roy was determined. He moved out of his father's house and roomed with three other truck drivers in a family hotel near downtown Los Angeles. Roy had always been an avid reader of the movie fan magazines, and he admitted to a reporter, "Believe it or not, I was so naïve I *believed* all those stories about people being discovered." So he parked his truck near the back gates of movie studios and stood outside, nervously smoking a cigarette. As you can imagine, nothing happened.

Roy was getting a lot of coaching, from his roommates and other acquaintances. First, he should have some photographs taken. Roy did so—twenty-five dollars for five poses. He sent them around to the studios. No response. Second, he had to look like an actor. He saved forty dollars from his truck driver's salary to buy a gabardine suit, the first real suit he had ever owned.

"I hear they are casting at Selznick," a fellow truck driver told Roy. He put on his gabardine suit and drove to Culver City for the most momentous meeting of his life, with Selznick's talent agent, Henry Willson.

Henry was immediately enthralled with the big, rawboned kid from Winnetka. They made a deal that day: Henry, who was planning to leave Selznick to form his own agency, would manage the young man, who would do exactly what Henry told him. Every day Roy underwent vocal training to eliminate his Midwestern accent and lower his voice to a resonant tone. Roy's prominent eyetooth was capped, and he learned to ride a horse, fence, tap-dance, wear a tuxedo, and adopt a ramrod posture.

Roy Fitzgerald also needed a new name.

"I always give a green actor the gimmick of a trick name to help him get known while he's learning his trade," Henry told *Look* magazine. "I named Guy Madison for a signboard advertising Dolly Madison cakes—all that boy thinks about is food. Tab Hunter's name came because I couldn't think of anything to tab him. As for Rock, I tried to think of something big and strong—Rock of Gibraltar. Hudson came from the Hudson River, for no reason. I knew that was it: Rock Hudson."

Thus the pattern was established from the outset: Henry Willson as the mastermind, calling all the shots, Rock as his consenting Galatea.

Henry had no luck in selling Rock Hudson to the studios, but he convinced the veteran director Raoul Walsh to put the young man under personal contract. A year later, Walsh cast his protégé in a war movie he was making for Warner Brothers, *Fighter Squadron*. The director gave Rock one line: "Pretty soon we're going to have to get a bigger blackboard." Rock required thirty-eight takes before he got it right.

Raoul Walsh and Henry Willson had invested nine thousand dollars in Rock's career, with no payoff. Henry tried to peddle his young actor at MGM, 20th Century-Fox, and other major studios, but he was turned down. Either Rock froze during an interview, or the studio balked at buying out Walsh's contract. The director suggested that Universal might be interested; the studio was struggling and needed new talent. Universal agreed to take over Walsh's contract, and Rock Hudson was signed to a seven-year contract starting at one hundred and fifty dollars a week.

His first assignment was a ten-second appearance in

Bright Victory. Rock studied drama in the classes of the studio coach, Sophie Rosenstein, and his roles began to grow. The fan magazines discovered him, thanks to the Universal publicity department, and their stories detailed his romances with Vera-Ellen, Piper Laurie, Marilyn Maxwell, and the script supervisor Betty Abbott.

As his fan mail grew, so did Rock's movie roles. He survived such films as *I Was a Shoplifter, The Desert Hawk, Shakedown, The Fat Man, Here Come the Nelsons,* and *Scarlet Angel.* The turning point came when Rock was given fourth billing in *Bend of the River,* starring James Stewart. At the premiere in Oregon, the young spectators screamed "Rock Hudson! Rock Hudson!" and ignored Stewart. The Universal executives took notice.

Thereafter Rock was starred in films. The movie that put him in the top rank of stars was *Magnificent Obsession.* It was released at about the time I met him.

4

Fling with a Movie Star

HE CERTAINLY DIDN'T DRESS like a movie star. Light blue denim slacks, a short-sleeved plaid cotton shirt, moccasins with sweat socks at half-mast.

"Henry wanted me to come in and sign some papers," he explained rather shyly. As if he needed an excuse to be there.

"Oh, yes, Mr. Willson is expecting you," I said in my most secretary-like manner. "Please go right in."

He ambled into Henry's office, and I tried not to stare.

Pat noticed my reaction, and she laughed, "Handsome, isn't he?"

I shook my head in astonishment. "I've never seen such long legs. Amazing!"

After a half hour's conference, Rock departed. Henry

emerged from his office beaming. "Well, what did you think of my number-one client?" he asked.

"Terrific," I replied in total honesty.

A few days later, Henry asked me to join him for cocktails after work at the Cock 'n Bull. That surprised me, because Henry rarely invited me for a social occasion; whenever we went to a restaurant or bar, it was always to meet a client or a producer. "By the way," Henry added, "Rock's coming by."

Naturally the invitation appealed to me. Henry and I walked across the street, and he led me to his usual table in a corner of the bar. Within a few minutes, the front door of the restaurant opened, and Rock's huge figure was silhouetted against the sunshine outside. He advanced toward our table, but the barroom was dark, and he stumbled over a chair, nearly landing on the floor.

Rock was laughing hilariously when he reached us. "Did you see that?" he said, laughing some more.

"Rock, it's not that funny," snapped Henry like a mother chastising an unruly child. I thought it was rather dear that a movie star could appear so awkward.

Henry started talking, and Rock and I listened. Henry was a vivid conversationalist who didn't require any feedback. Some of what he said was trade talk that I didn't fully understand. Most of the time he darted from one subject to another, telling a racy piece of gossip, relating the latest off-color joke, deriding actors who were not his clients, delivering his reviews of the latest movies. Occasionally he paused and directed a question at me: "What do you think of this crazy Hollywood scene, Phyllis?" He didn't always wait for an answer.

At six-thirty Henry glanced at his watch and said, "Why don't we all go over to Frascati's for dinner? Are you free, Phyllis?"

Was I free? To have dinner with Rock Hudson? My heart was skipping a beat or two as I hurried to my apartment on Fairfax Avenue, took a quick shower, and picked out a fresh dress that I thought would look attractive in the candle-light at Frascati's. It was a warm, quiet place with friendly waitresses and hearty Belgian food. Henry and Rock were already there when I arrived, and we had another round of drinks before ordering dinner. Again Henry occupied center stage while Rock and I listened with amusement. Three times Henry left the table to make telephone calls and twice he was summoned to the phone. During his absences, Rock and I made clumsy attempts at small talk. I discovered that Rock Hudson in person was nothing like Rock Hudson the self-assured hero of the movie screen. He was terribly shy, and since I myself was not a tower of self-confidence, it didn't make for sparkling conversation. But as long as Henry was at the table, we had a marvelous time.

The next morning I picked up the office phone and heard the familiar warm voice, "Hi, this is Rock."

"Oh, good morning," I said, attempting to sound businesslike. "Just a minute, I'll put Mr. Willson on."

"No, wait a minute. I want to talk to you. How about dinner Friday night?"

I was overwhelmed. "Sure. What time will you pick me up?"

"About seven. See you then."

I put down the receiver and sat for a moment in wonderment. "Can you believe that?" I said to Pat Devlin.

"Believe what?"

"Rock Hudson just asked me to dinner Friday night."

"You mean on business?"

"No, it's just a date."

"A date with Rock Hudson! Do you realize what millions of girls would do for that?"

Did I! It was absolutely unbelievable. I was actually being asked out on a date with one of the most desirable men in America. All at once I started wondering: What shall I wear? Where will we go? What could I talk about that would interest him? I was walking on air for two days.

I came down to earth on Thursday. Rock was on the

phone: "Gee, Phyllis, I'm really sorry, but I can't keep our date tomorrow night. The studio has scheduled a fan magazine layout, and I can't get out of it. I'll call you next week."

He did call the following week to make a date. Which he broke. When the same thing happened a third time, I walked into Henry's office and complained, "I don't enjoy having people make dates with me and then cancel them. Tell your number-one client to stop bothering me."

"Now calm down, sweetie," Henry said soothingly. "*I'll* take you to dinner. I'll admit I'm not Rock Hudson, but what the hell. Any old date in a storm."

Henry escorted me to a small French restaurant on Sunset Boulevard, and—surprise! Who should be sitting in another booth but Rock Hudson. He was being interviewed by a fan magazine writer, and Rock nodded sheepishly as Henry and I entered. Obviously this had been no coincidence. Henry was aware of Rock's whereabouts nearly every hour of the day. He had taken me to the restaurant to embarrass Rock.

Rock continued with the interview, but every few minutes he glanced over at me. I did my best to appear unperturbed, which was not difficult because Henry kept the conversation bubbling. Rock stopped by our table briefly, and I was calculatedly cool.

"Who needs actors?" I said to Pat Devlin the following morning. Both of us had seen actors at their best and at their worst as they paraded through the office. They were pretty to look at but, oh, they could be so vain and shallow and self-centered.

My own social life had improved greatly after a year in Los Angeles, thanks in large part to Pat. She frequently invited me to dinner at her parents' home in Westwood. They were a warm, convivial, Irish family, and I often accompanied them to dinner at the Bel Air Country Club. Through Pat I met and dated Travis Kleefield, a man-about-town who squired Jane Wyman, Ann Miller, and other actresses. He was a charmer, the first man who ever sent me a dozen red roses.

I had put Rock Hudson out of my mind. Or so I told myself. I had no time to waste on big-headed movie actors who broke dates as casually as they would light cigarettes.

Ten days before Christmas I had a chance encounter that was to change the course of my life. I decided that my first California Christmas would be a festive one, if only for myself. I was going to decorate my apartment in grand style, or at least as grand as the five-and-dime store in my neighborhood would allow. I was staring at the decorations when I nearly collided with another shopper.

"Hi, Phyllis, how've you been?"

I gazed skyward, into the face of Rock Hudson. His smile was so incandescent that I forgot my resentment over his no-shows, though I was determined not to appear overeager about seeing him again.

"Doing a little Christmas shopping?" he asked.

"As you can see."

"Oh, you know Craig Hill, don't you?"

I gazed at his companion and recognized Craig. He was another of Henry's young clients, an incredibly handsome young man with the looks of a surfer—tan skin, blond hair, and eyes the color of the Pacific. Rock seemed flustered as he introduced Craig. We exchanged greetings, and the three of us muttered clichés about Christmas shopping.

"I'll call you tomorrow," said Rock as he and Craig departed.

Oh, sure, I said under my breath.

He did telephone me at the office the following morning. "How about having dinner with me tonight at the Villa Nova?" he asked.

"Sounds okay," I said.

When I told Henry about the invitation, he was enthusiastic. "Great! I'll join you. I've got a new client I want Rock to meet. And I want to talk to Rock about some business matters."

The Villa Nova, an Italian restaurant with booths conducive to romance, was across from the office on Sunset Boulevard. Henry, his client, and I met Rock there, and any potential for romance was drowned by a flood of silly talk. The three men maintained a giddy conversation of total trivia, laughing merrily at their lame *bons mots.* I finally gave up trying to join in. I could hardly wait to leave the dinner and return to my apartment.

Rock and Henry must have sensed my discomfort. As soon as I arrived in the office the following morning, Rock was on the phone.

"Hi," he said in that baritone that could melt a glacier. "How would you like to go dancing Friday night?"

"Sounds like fun. Where?"

"Henry told me about a new room on top of the Beverly Hilton. It's called L'Escoffier Room."

"Sounds awfully fancy."

On my lunch hour I hurried over to Saks and picked out a black evening dress. I didn't buy it at first because it was expensive, and I wanted to make sure Rock wasn't going to cancel again. When I told Henry and Pat Devlin about my forthcoming date, they were excited. Pat told me that her parents had been to L'Escoffier and had been impressed. "I'll tell you how fancy it is," Pat said. "They don't even have prices on the menu."

"Fine!" said Henry. "Tell them to give you a bill without numbers."

For two days I answered the telephone with apprehension, fearing that it would be Rock saying, "Sorry, I gotta do a fan magazine interview that night." The call never came. Precisely at seven on Friday, Rock appeared at my door looking heavenly in a dark blue suit, white shirt, and red-and-navy striped tie. He was every inch the movie star.

Rock acted like some of the dates I'd had in high school. He took my arm and escorted me to his Buick convertible. He opened the door, waited until I was seated, then gently closed it. He did everything but present a corsage.

He was just as beautifully mannered at L'Escoffier. He nodded graciously as the excited maître d' led us to a choice table. He ordered a Scotch and soda for each of us, then selected a vintage Beaujolais to accompany the dinner. He volunteered to order for us, a chore I willingly surrendered. First came baked potatoes with sour cream and caviar in the middle. The main course was prime rib, medium rare, with salad following the entrée, continental style.

Rock, who had often been tongue-tied and clumsy during the times I had seen him, was suddenly a witty conversationalist. He told me stories about his trip to Ireland for *Captain Lightfoot,* including the time he found pizza in Dublin. He said that one night he had an overwhelming urge for pizza. "There is no pizza in Ireland," insisted his dialogue coach, Charles FitzSimons. But Rock found an old news vendor who happened to be Italian and who directed him to an Italian restaurant. "I was even able to find peanut butter in Ireland," Rock said proudly.

Rock talked a great deal about the big meals he consumed in Ireland—surprisingly, he actually lost weight, probably because the movie was so strenuous. He told of climbing to the top of Blarney Castle with Betty Abbott and Barbara Rush. They were too exhausted and afraid of the height, but Rock leaned back and down and kissed the stone. I gathered from his conversation that he had spent a lot of time touring the sights with Betty. But I had heard through Henry that Rock had also toured Europe with Barbara Rush, who was then having problems with her marriage to Jeffrey Hunter.

After the first course, Joe Moshay and his musicians assembled on the bandstand and began playing a lilting melody. Rock nodded toward the dance floor, and I smiled my assent. There may have been others there, but as far as I was concerned, Rock and I were performing by ourselves. He was the best dancer I had ever known, enveloping me gently in his arms, leading me over the floor in perfect rhythm, masterful but not overwhelming. My only problem was a stiff neck the following morning from gazing upward at his face.

He brought me home at midnight and gave me a warm kiss on the doorstep. I lay in bed sleepless for an hour, savoring the pleasures of the evening. Still, my Midwestern conservatism interrupted with the caution: "Now, Phyllis, don't overdo. Just because you had one lovely date with a movie star doesn't mean anything more serious is going to follow. Go to sleep now." But of course I couldn't sleep. I was restless all night.

The warmth of the memories remained with me on Saturday as I pursued the chores I had postponed during the workweek. I was finishing my ironing when I heard a knock at the door. I opened it and stared at a seven-foot Christmas tree. "What do you think of it?" said a voice. Then I saw Rock's face peering through the foliage. He was grinning from ear to ear, like a kid who had discovered a great new toy.

"Why—why, it's beautiful!" I said, catching my breath.

"I've got loads of decorations in the car," Rock said excitedly.

Somehow he managed to shove the tree into my apartment. "But where are we going to put it?" I said.

"There—right in the corner," he said, struggling. My living room looked like another part of the forest when he got it located. "See—it fits!" he said. By this time, his sweatshirt was covered with pine needles.

The tree didn't exactly fit, but Rock trimmed a few inches off the top. I put some records on the phonograph, and we danced around the room in a repeat of our performance at L'Escoffier. Rock had no trouble stringing lights and attaching ornaments at the top of the tree; I took care of the bottom half.

At eight in the evening both of us remembered we were hungry and we walked around the corner to a hamburger place. Back in the apartment, we danced once more, then sat on the couch and watched the lights blink on the Christmas tree. Rock had been talking almost nonstop since he arrived with the tree, telling stories about the location in Ireland, about working there with crusty old Raoul Walsh, the one-eyed director who had discovered Rock for films. I had never seen Rock so animated.

Suddenly he stopped talking and stared at me with a quizzical, little-boy grin. He leaned his head toward mine, and our lips brushed tantalizingly. He kissed me. His lips were soft and pliant and thrilling. The kiss lasted a long time, and I didn't want it to end. His big hands were amazingly gentle as he began to explore, and I fell completely under his spell. He was masterful, yet tender, and he had a magnificent body.

The love act itself was sublimely passionate, though it ended sooner than I would have liked. I figured Rock had been overly excited. Soon he was sleeping like a baby— Rock Hudson naked in my bed. I contemplated that perfect face, that long but ideally proportioned body. How easy it would be to fall in love with him. Or had I already?

Calm yourself, Phyllis. Take it slow, I thought. This is what movie stars are notorious for: one-night stands with compliant girls. I steadied myself and tried to reason that this was just an actor's fling. Having made the conquest, he might never call me again.

But something inside wasn't buying that.

A DAY LATER, Rock telephoned me and said, "Could I spend Christmas Eve with you? I don't have any place to go."

How touching, I thought. Rock was well on his way to becoming one of the most famous men in the world, yet he had no one to be with on Christmas Eve.

"Of course," I replied.

I had already accepted an invitation from Pat Devlin's parents to join them, Pat, and her brother Jack for Christmas Eve dinner at the Bel Air Country Club. When I told Pat how sorry I felt for Rock, she said immediately, "You'd be crazy not to go with him."

Rock arrived on Christmas Eve with his arms filled with presents. "I've been shopping for two days," he said with a child's excitement. Fortunately I had taken time off from work to buy him some things too. He carefully laid his presents under my huge tree, then shook the packages that I had marked for him.

We dined at a small French restaurant on Sunset Boulevard, a dark place with candles on every table. Christmas carols were being played on the loudspeaker, and it seemed a perfect place for a Christmas Eve dinner. I ordered duck à l'orange and Rock had beef bourguignon. The food was delicious.

I expected Rock to be as cheerful and exuberant as he had been three nights before, but he wasn't. He seemed depressed, and he had little to say. After a couple of glasses of Beaujolais, his spirits improved. He asked me if I wanted to have Christmas dinner with his mother and stepfather, and I accepted. As we drank coffee after dinner, he again became preoccupied. I couldn't seem to penetrate that curtain of gloom. Was he remembering other Christmases of a lonely childhood? Was something about his career bothering him? He gave no hint, and I didn't feel I should invade his privacy.

Rock's mood switched as we approached my apartment. Now he was a boy again, filled with the anticipation of Christmas. He gathered his presents for me from under the tree and laid them at my feet. He studied my face expectantly as I opened each package. The presents were beautiful: a white silk blouse, quilted navy skirt, navy shoes, navy purse.

"What exquisite taste!" I exclaimed sincerely. "But how on earth did you know my sizes?"

Rock smiled. "A little bird told me."

"Could that little bird be named Pat Devlin?"

"Well, yes. But all the selections were mine."

Rock expressed delight with what I had bought him: a beige cashmere sweater, beige desert boots, and a pipe. Again we made love and he stayed all night.

In the morning Rock didn't feel like returning to his place at the Shoreham Apartments. He went next door to borrow a razor from John Smith, a Henry Willson client who had moved into the apartment building two weeks before. We both donned our Christmas outfits and set out for Christmas dinner in Pasadena. Astonishingly, it was snowing, though not much. It melted soon after hitting the pavement—nothing like the full-textured snow I had known in Minnesota. I had always believed that it never snowed in Los Angeles, but there it was, falling on the freeway on Christmas Day.

KAY AND JOE OLSEN lived in a modest bungalow in a middle-class section of Pasadena. Kay was a large woman, tall and full-bosomed, obviously the dominant force in the household. Joe was a pleasant, smiling man who seemed to hang on his wife's every word. Joe was the third of her husbands, maybe the fourth. After Roy Scherer and Wallace Fitzgerald, I understand there was another husband before Joe, but nobody talked about him. Rock seemed to enjoy Joe Olsen, but they really had little in common.

Kay had invited two neighboring couples to the Christmas dinner, and she enjoyed the awe with which they regarded her son the movie star. During the afternoon I was amazed by the relationship between mother and son.

"Does Rock want a turkey leg? I know it's his favorite piece."

"Yes, Mom, a turkey leg. You bet!"

Or, "How about another scoop of dressing for my baby boy?"

Rock flashed a wide grin and nodded his head. Kay continued serving him until he had consumed three full servings. She beamed at him with almost every bite. It was a delicious meal, served with wine, the best home-cooked meal I'd enjoyed since leaving Minnesota. After dinner, we women cleared the plates and washed them, then Kay served pumpkin pie, whipped cream, and coffee. Everyone groaned happily over the sumptuous feast. During the final cleanup, the men retired to the living room, and I was delighted to see Rock light up his Christmas pipe.

"Rock, tell the neighbors about your wonderful trip to Ireland," Kay told her son.

"Tell the folks about the new movie you're going to make, Rock." All of Kay's attention focused on her son, and she spoke to him as if she were talking to a small boy. To my amazement, Rock responded almost in a kind of baby talk.

Rock and I left the Olsen house about five o'clock, and as we drove back to Los Angeles I felt happy. Rock didn't. He was in a funk again.

Finally he said, "I hate what she does."

"Your mother?"

"She's more like a fan than a mother."

I decided not to pursue the matter, and we continued along the freeway in silence.

I WENT TO WORK as usual Monday morning and did my customary chores of opening the office: adjusting the heat, making coffee, sorting out the mail, checking the answering service, reviewing the trade papers. As I glanced over Mike Connolly's column in *Hollywood Reporter,* my eye stopped at this item: "Rock Hudson has been enjoying hideaway dinners with Henry Willson's purty secy. Phyllis Gates."

Hmmm, so our little affair was now public knowledge. I wondered how Connolly got his hands on that piece of information. I didn't have to wonder long. I knew that Henry and Mike were close buddies. Whenever Henry had some news that he wanted made known to the trade, he could always count on Connolly, whose gossip column was read by everyone in Hollywood.

Contrary to the Connolly item, I was no longer just a secretary. Henry had given me a subagent's license as a Christmas present. The promotion was not accompanied by a raise, however.

I continued seeing Rock, but he was busy at the studio with looping for *Captain Lightfoot* and catching up on the fan magazine assignments that had accumulated during his absence abroad. He sometimes had dinner with Henry or with Barbara Rush and Jeff Hunter. On days off, he relaxed beside Henry's pool in Stone Canyon.

Meanwhile he was shopping for a house, the first he would ever own. It would turn out to be the house where I would know my utmost happiness and my greatest sorrow and where, after a lapse of twenty-five years, I still live when I am in Los Angeles.

5

"Let Me Take Care of You"

"I FOUND IT! I found it! It's perfect, just what I need. You gotta come see it. You gotta!"

"Wait a minute," I said. "Slow down. What is it you found?"

"The house of my dreams!" Rock enthused. "I want you to be the first person to see it. I'll show it to you right now!"

"Rock, I'm working. I can't just pick up and leave the office."

"It's only five minutes away. Henry won't mind if you leave the office for a few minutes."

"Tell you what. Pick me up at twelve noon. I'll go on my lunch hour. I'll be standing out in front."

His enthusiasm was really quite endearing. When he stopped his convertible in front of the office, I had never seen him so excited. You'd think he had just won an Oscar.

Rock speeded up Doheny Drive, screeching his tires at every turn. We sailed past all the bird streets—Oriole, Mockingbird, Flicker, Robin, etc.—then turned on Sparrow Lane. It's a tiny street, less than half a block. Rock drove up a steep driveway, and we arrived in front of his dream house.

It looked like a cabin in the mountains. Tall pine trees stood like sentinels all around it. Behind the house, a slope rose three hundred feet almost straight up; it was covered with ivy, with footpaths angling through it. The house was rustic with heavy beams and shake roof. The outer walls were painted barn red.

The real estate agent had left the door ajar, and Rock excitedly led me inside. I could see immediately why he had been charmed by the house. It was warm and inviting, with burnished floors of pegged and grooved oak in intricate patterns. The living room had a pine provincial mantel and a matching bar. The kitchen, compact, serviceable, also had pine cupboards.

"Look at that barbecue!" Rock said. It was indeed a handsome barbecue, floor to ceiling, in red brick.

He showed me the two small bedrooms and the bathroom.

"It's not a big place, but it's all I need."

He continued the tour, taking me to the back patio where slices of tree trunks formed a path. With the pine trees and the sharply rising mountainside, the place seemed like a refuge in the woods.

"Are you going to buy it?" I asked.

"Sure!" he said. "It's only thirty-two thousand. Henry says I can swing that. And what a location! I can drive to Universal in fifteen minutes. The same with any of the studios. I couldn't find a more central place."

His enthusiasm was infectious. "How wonderful for you, Rock," I said. "I know you'll be very happy here."

"Phyllis?"

"Yes."

"Come live with me here. Quit your job, move in. Let me take care of you."

I was thunderstruck. Speechless. I couldn't believe what I had heard. Nothing Rock had said or done had prepared me for this. He had never said he loved me. He had never given any indication that I was any different in his life from the other women he had dated in Hollywood. He seemed to enjoy my company and the fact that I was unimpressed by his stardom. But living together? I had never contemplated the possibility of living with a man to whom I wasn't married. And I certainly couldn't consider it now, even though I felt a growing affection—call it love—for Rock.

I said to Rock, "You're sweet, but I don't think I'm ready for something like that. I like my job, and I like the way things are between us now."

Rock seemed to accept my answer. I couldn't tell whether he was serious in wanting to make our relationship more substantial, or whether he thought a house should have a woman in it, to cook and sew and clean up, the way his mother always did. At any rate, he made the deal for the house and waited with great impatience for the escrow to close.

WHEN HE WASN'T WORKING, Rock was a mess. He didn't know what to do with himself. Work was everything to him; he had no hobbies. I encouraged him to take up tennis, but he said he felt like a klutz on the court. He didn't like people to see him make a fool of himself. I took him golfing a couple of times, but that didn't work. He couldn't give the ball a solid hit, and he couldn't tolerate the fact that my score was better than his.

The only thing that absorbed him while he wasn't working was fan magazine interviews. Betty Mitchell of the Universal publicity department called him almost every day with a new interview, and Rock accepted all of them. "Those magazines paid attention to me when I was making all those crummy pictures at Universal," he said. "I owe it to 'em."

I was seeing Rock a couple times a week. Sometimes I cooked dinner at his Shoreham apartment, sometimes we sent out for pizza. It wasn't easy to be around him during those nonworking periods. His mood swings ranged from sheer exhilaration to black depression. "What's the matter, Rock?" I asked him. "Tell me what's troubling you."

"Nothing, nothing," he said, fading once more into a dark mood.

Those periods of depression alarmed me. I had never known anyone whose very nature could alter so abruptly. There seemed to be two Rock Hudsons: the affable, grinning charmer he portrayed so brilliantly on the screen; and the dour, gloomy person he revealed to me. During those low periods, he seemed almost overcome with self-loathing. I couldn't reach him. I could only wait until he climbed out of the pit and returned to his usual self.

Rock didn't care too much for the company of other actors—too much competition perhaps. George Nader was an exception. George was a rising young actor at Universal, getting the same kind of romantic buildup that Rock had been given. George was not as tall as Rock, but he had a better physique, being muscular and athletic, which Rock was not. He was a rugged-looking former Navy officer with wavy hair and a friendly smile.

One day Rock announced that we were going to have dinner at George's house. I had met George three months earlier, and I enjoyed his marvelous sense of humor. On the drive to the San Fernando Valley, Rock told me that I would be meeting another friend named Mark Miller. He explained that Mark had once had ambitions of being a singer or actor, but had given it up to become George's business manager. "You'll like Mark," Rock said. "He's a lot of fun."

The evening with George and Mark was indeed enjoyable—up to a point. George was a great storyteller; he delighted in reporting inside secrets about other Universal actors. I loved to hear him tell about studio happenings, something I could never get Rock to do. Mark could also be unusually witty, and we laughed our way through the evening.

But then Mark said, "Let's play charades."

George and Rock were delighted with the idea, and nobody listened to my groan of disapproval.

It wasn't fair. George and Rock were actors, and Mark seemed to like playacting, too. That left me, a farm girl with a streak of shyness despite my self-assured manner. The evening ended with much laughter as the three men hooted at my attempts to act out the phrases I had been given.

Rock's morale rose after he closed the escrow and moved into the house on Sparrow Lane. He brought along his prized possessions: a king-size bed and his hi-fi set. His idea of furnishing was to move the outdoor furniture inside. The dinner table was a long redwood table with two redwood benches. For sitting, two redwood lounge chairs. That was it. "I don't need anything else," he claimed.

On February 7, 1955, Rock took me to a preview of *Captain Lightfoot*. He looked heavenly in his military uniform, but the movie was nothing to shout about. On March 19, Rock began filming *Never Say Goodbye* at the studio. His costars were the German actress Cornell Borchers and George Sanders. Rock was always happiest when he was making a movie, and I was glad to see the end of his silent moods.

Never Say Goodbye was another Universal potboiler aimed at capitalizing on the studio's most valuable star. But the greatest opportunity of Rock's career was just around the corner.

"ROCK, GEORGE STEVENS wants to see you," Henry Willson said excitedly.

Rock was his phlegmatic self on the other end of the telephone. "Yeah, what about?"

"Giant, for crissake."

"What's that? Some kind of science fiction movie?"

"Jesus, how dumb can you be? It's the Edna Ferber novel about Texas. George has been talking to a lot of stars, from Bill Holden to Greg Peck. Now he's decided to cast younger actors and make them age instead of having older actors play it young in the early parts. He's already signed Elizabeth Taylor."

"Elizabeth Taylor, huh? Sounds interesting."

"Now I gotta find a way to get Universal to lend you to Warner Brothers."

Henry found a way, and he was insufferable around the office for weeks. You'd think he had swung the biggest deal since the Louisiana Purchase. "This is it!" he kept saying. "This is going to be an Academy Award for Rock!"

Rock himself was excited. This time he was really climbing up in class, working with one of the screen's great directors and with a topflight cast headed by Elizabeth Taylor and the brilliant newcomer James Dean. The only part that Rock wasn't thrilled about was Dean. He was the new kid on the block, hailed as the next Brando after *East of Eden.* Dean was a Method actor out of the Actors Studio. Rock's only training was with Sophie Rosenstein at Universal.

Rock had known Jimmy Dean slightly. Three years before, Dean had played a bit part in *Has Anybody Seen My Gal?* in which Rock starred with Piper Laurie. Rock knew that he and Elizabeth Taylor had the major roles in *Giant,* but Dean as the flamboyant wildcatter Jett Rink could divert attention to himself. It was the first time in Rock's career that he had faced a threat from another actor, and he was disturbed by it.

ROCK'S CAREER was ascending fast. The fan magazines clamored for interviews, and Rock cooperated with all of them. Universal was making millions from its young star, and the studio was beginning to show a degree of appreciation.

"You can't do magazine layouts at your house when all you've got is redwood outdoor furniture," a studio executive told him. "We'll furnish your house."

Universal hired the prestigious store, W&J Sloane, to decorate Rock's house. "You talk to them," Rock told me. "I don't know anything about furnishing."

I realized the furniture had to be large—to fit Rock. Working with the Sloane decorator, I chose a large red sectional for the living room and a five-foot round travertine marble table for the dining area. Rock agreed with all my choices except for the rugs.

"I like rag rugs," Rock said.

"I hate rag rugs," I replied. "We should have a carpet to make the house warmer. It's awfully cold."

We argued and argued, and I finally won. I chose a thick wool beige carpeting which was laid in all the rooms. We were both wrong. The Sparrow house had—and still has—beautiful pegged-wood floors that shouldn't be covered.

Rock wanted everything in the house to be macho—guns over the mantel and all that. I put my foot down. If I ever did move in with him—something I had not yet reconciled myself to—I couldn't see myself living in a hunting lodge.

Rock was pleased with the final result, and the house added to his sense of well-being. For the first time in his life he was enjoying a measure of confidence in himself and his career. He wanted nothing—absolutely nothing—to interfere with his future.

6

Giant and
James Dean

ROCK FINISHED HIS WORK in *Never Say Goodbye* and left immediately for Charlottesville, Virginia, to film the first locations for *Giant.* He telephoned me with glowing reports of the lush pastures, the white rail fences, the beautiful thoroughbred horses, the stately houses. "Even the motel where I'm staying looks like a colonial mansion," he said.

I missed Rock terribly when he was in Virginia and I stayed home almost every night waiting for his call. He was so excited about filming *Giant,* and I enjoyed hearing about everything that was going on. Sometimes I would close my eyes and try to imagine the Virginia countryside. Rock was very happy during this time. He knew this was his big break.

But things were different when he moved to the major

location at Marfa, Texas. He hated the heat and the dust. He hated his accommodations and the location food. Most of all, he hated James Dean. He thought Dean was a poseur and a malingerer. And Rock was convinced that George Stevens was spending more time with Dean so that Dean could steal the picture.

Rock's complaints upset Henry.

"Isn't that just like an actor!" Henry exclaimed. "I get him the best role of his lifetime, and all he can do is complain. Phyllis, I want you to go down there and see what's going on. See if you can't calm him down. I know you can do it. You have a certain spell over Rock. I've noticed."

I suppose I blushed a little. It was nice to know that I had some kind of effect on Rock. But I certainly didn't want to go off to some godforsaken spot in the middle of Texas and get involved with a lot of high-powered personalities. And yet I really missed Rock and longed to see him again.

"I'll go," I said.

"Fine. Here's your train ticket."

I still didn't know where our romance would lead, if anywhere. And I knew that, although absence may make the heart grow fonder, absence on a movie location, with all its distractions and temptations, can be risky.

I hate trains. My stint with the airline had made me appreciate fast travel, so I got no enjoyment from the long train ride through mile after mile of arid flatland. When I arrived in midafternoon and stepped down to the platform in the dry, stifling heat, a young man came forward and took my suitcase.

"Hi, you're Phyllis, aren't you? I'm Dennis Hopper. Rock is working today, so I'm the reception committee. I'll take you to your hotel."

He was a polite, clean-cut man in his early twenties. As we drove to the hotel in the location car, he told me he was going crazy with so much time on his hands. He was playing the son of Rock and Elizabeth Taylor in the latter part of the movie, and his scenes hadn't started yet. He left me

at the hotel, and I unpacked and took a walk around the
town. There wasn't much to see but grain stores and hard-
wares and roadside cafés.

AT SIX O'CLOCK I heard a knock at my door.

"Hi, Bunting, welcome to Texas," Rock grinned, using
his favorite name for me. (I never knew where he got it,
maybe from the nursery rhyme, "Bye, Baby Bunting.") He
lifted me in his long arms, carried me to the bed, and
started making love. He was overwhelming, as passionate
as he had ever been.

Almost immediately afterward, Rock said, "C'mon, let's
go see the dailies."

He told me that every night before dinner, George Stevens watched the dailies with the cast and key members of
the crew in a hotel banquet hall that had been converted
into a projection room. They had already started when we
arrived, and Rock and I fumbled in the dark to find seats.
Everyone was silent, awaiting the leader's succinct com-
ments. Rock was enraptured by what he watched on the
screen. I thought it was boring to see the same scene over
and over again with no discernible variation. Stevens was
notorious for the number of takes that he had printed.

When the lights went up, I found myself surrounded by
strangers, many of them famous. Rock introduced me—
somewhat proudly, I thought—to George Stevens, whose
friendly manner contrasted with his reputation as a tough
man on a movie set. He welcomed me to the *Giant* location
and introduced me to his son and assistant, George, Jr. I felt
a warm glow as Rock clutched me around the shoulders
and showed me off to his friends and coworkers.

"This is Elizabeth," said Rock, as if I needed to be told.
There was no mistaking the violet eyes, the flawless beauty.
She gave me a pleasant hello, then went into a conference
with the director.

Rock introduced me to other members of the cast: Mercedes McCambridge, Chill Wills, Jane Withers, Sal Mineo, Carroll Baker, Fran Bennett. Also James Dean. He was small and exceedingly shy. He gave me a weak handshake and then disappeared. All of us went into dinner in the hotel dining room. A catering service from Hollywood prepared the meals, and they were first-class, which, I learned, was the only way George Stevens operated. Most of the company went to bed early, because shooting began early and the days were long.

I slept late the next morning, still exhausted from the train ride. The commissary crew served me breakfast—they were open all day to accommodate crew members. I walked out and into the hot Texas morning and saw James Dean spinning a lariat on the sidewalk. He started with a small loop, then spun and spun until he had a large loop.

"Mornin', ma'am," he said in his Texas drawl. Dean, like all the *Giant* actors, had been trained in the accent by Bob Hinkle, an ex-rodeo star who spoke pure Texan.

"Like to try this?" Dean asked.

"Yup," I answered, trying to match his accent.

He put the rope in my hands, then stood behind me and held my arms so I could follow his movements. We had a lot of laughs over my attempts. Finally he put his arm around my shoulders and said, "Well, little lady, let's go to the commissary and have some of that Texas chili."

It was a bit soon after breakfast, but I was willing to give it a try. As we were entering the dining room, I overheard Jane Withers tell a companion, "I can't understand what Rock is going to do with her here." I didn't get the import of her remark until later.

Dean and I conversed during lunch—I just had some chili, which was very, very hot—and we talked about mundane matters. He was not the kind of person you could get close to, and that was the only time I spent alone with him. He was the loner of the *Giant* company. When he wasn't working on the set, he drove his Jeep into the desert and shot jackrabbits. It seemed senseless to me, killing all those harmless animals. But Dean arrived back in Marfa in the evening with a Jeep full. He even went into the desert at night, shone a spotlight on the rabbits to "freeze" them, then shot them.

JAMES DEAN was the main subject of Rock's complaints. Rock was sharing a house with Dean and Chill Wills, and Rock grumbled that his costar was a slob.

"Stevens is throwing the picture to Dean, I know he is," Rock complained. "Dammit, he spends all his time talking to Dean, and he hardly tells me a thing."

"Maybe he has more confidence in you," I said consolingly, "and he figures Dean needs more direction. After all, this is only Jimmy's third picture. You've done more than thirty."

"I need as much direction as he does. I've never worked with someone of Stevens's caliber before. I've worked with hacks, mostly. Stevens is giving Dean all the closeups. I'm left out in the cold."

Rock seemed very insecure to me. He let Henry take care of everything. I couldn't understand why he didn't assume any personal responsibility—my mother had always taught us to make our own decisions.

Nothing I said could assuage Rock's jealousy of Jimmy Dean. Rock was angry that he had to work so hard at acting while it came easily to Dean. He resented the fact that visiting press concentrated on Dean as the new sensation in films. He was upset because teenagers visiting the set squealed when Dean came in view. Rock's resentment turned into active hatred. Rock was determined to be well prepared, and he came to my room after dinner to practice his lines for the following day. I read the dialogue of Elizabeth Taylor and James Dean while Rock delivered his own lines.

"Would you like to visit the location tomorrow?" he asked.

"Sure," I said.

"Wear something cool. It's gonna be hotter'n hell out there."

I wore a black-and-white cotton dress, which was perfect, and sandals, which were not. With all the dirt and insects, I should have had boots. We drove for miles and miles over the flat plain, devoid of anything but fences. Then in the distance I could see, rising out of the flatness like a vision, the big Victorian mansion that George Stevens had built in the middle of nowhere.

George Stevens, dressed in cowboy hat, plaid shirt, and jeans, welcomed me to the set. I was amazed that he would go out of his way to do that, since he was managing a couple hundred people on a complex location. But that was the kind of man he was, warm and thoughtful.

As soon as we got out of the car, Rock started taking movies of me. Just before starting *Giant*, he had bought a Bolex movie camera, and he was like a kid with a new toy. He took reels and reels of film, of me talking to the actors, of sunrises and sunsets, of dust blowing. The camera became an obsession with him.

Remembering our lariat spinning, I gave James Dean a cordial "How are you today?" He gave the front of his Stetson a pull, gazed over my shoulder, and mumbled, "Mornin', ma'am, good to see ya." Then he ambled away. He never even looked at me, but that was the way he talked to everybody.

Elizabeth Taylor and I chatted cordially, but it was apparent her mind was on other matters too. She soon gave all her attention to the hairdresser, the makeup man, the script clerk. These were the people she had spent most of her life with, her other family. She had little interest in anyone who wasn't in the movie business, like me. Naturally I felt resentful, but I was learning that actors didn't behave like other people.

Before I left Hollywood, someone had whispered to me that Rock and Elizabeth were having an affair. Elizabeth's husband, Michael Wilding, had stayed in California, and she found herself on a faraway location with two extremely attractive leading men. She seemed intrigued by the quirky charm of James Dean, but his remoteness precluded romance. What about Rock? He devoted much attention to Elizabeth. They were almost childish with each other, talking a kind of baby talk and playing pranks like throwing water at each other. Knowing how jealous Rock was of Dean, it wouldn't have surprised me if Rock had made a play for Elizabeth, hoping to maintain his balance of power in the *Giant* company. When I saw Rock and Elizabeth together, I understood the reason for Jane Withers's crack after I had arrived.

Was I jealous? Not really. I realized that no normal male could resist the fabulous charms of Elizabeth Taylor. I had no claim on Rock, no reason to be possessive. If there had been an affair, I doubted that it would last. I was content that Rock had, with his passionate welcome to Texas, demonstrated his feelings toward me.

I enjoyed watching Rock work, but the heat and sand were almost too much for me. I managed to survive the day only by consuming gallons of iced tea. On the drive back to Marfa, I mentioned that I'd like to visit Mexico, which I had never seen. Rock arranged for Dennis Hopper to drive me across the border, and we had a wonderful time poking around the shops and cantinas. Rock had given me money to buy silver things for his new house, and I found a pair of candlesticks that were stunning.

Five days after I arrived in Marfa, location filming was completed, and the company packed up for the return to Hollywood. Most of the company traveled by train, and Rock and I occupied a compartment. He left only for meals. Most of the time he watched the passing desert scene, or he complained.

"Dammit, this is getting to be Jimmy Dean's picture," he ranted. "They're all trying to screw me."

No amount of reassurance would change his sour mood. When I walked through the train to watch the poker games or chat with members of the crew, Rock objected. He didn't want me to mingle with the rest of the company. We did manage some lovemaking, my first on a train. It was wonderful.

SHORTLY AFTER WE RETURNED from Texas, Rock called me from the studio, which was something he rarely did.

"Elizabeth wants us to come to dinner tonight," he said.

"Both of us?"

"Of course. She said, 'Bring that nice Phyllis with you.' "

"But what do I wear?"

"She said to dress very casual."

I left the office early and went to my apartment to pick out a pair of summer slacks and a silk blouse, then I drove to Rock's house. I arrived as he was returning from Warner Brothers. He changed clothes and we rode west on Sunset Boulevard to Benedict Canyon, then climbed Tower Road.

Rock and I stepped inside the gate and entered a Hawaiian paradise. The azure pool was surrounded by lush tropical foliage and spotlighted in pastel shades. Michael Wilding greeted us at the door. He was a mild-mannered man in slacks and a short-sleeved summer shirt, with a scarf tied neatly around his neck in the manner of English actors. He led us inside to an elegantly furnished living room and asked our preference in drinks.

During the next hour we drank and talked and waited for Elizabeth. The two young Wilding sons, Michael and Christopher, did not appear, but several small, fluffy dogs ran around the room. Finally, Elizabeth made her entrance. Dress informally, she had said. She herself wore a lavender evening gown with several pounds of jewelry. The maid served us dinner on trays, and it was a cordial, get-acquainted evening that ended early because both Elizabeth and Rock had early calls.

A week later, I suggested to Rock that he invite Elizabeth and Michael to dinner. There were no servants to help entertain, but I had faith in my own ability as a cook, and figured the Wildings would simply have to accept us on our own terms.

I put a pork roast on the barbecue and prepared two vegetables and a savory salad. Both the Wildings raved over the meal, and Elizabeth said, "I can't believe you can cook!" Obviously she had never boiled an egg in her life. Universal, always eager to please its major star, had sent Rock a case of vintage French wine, and we managed to consume several bottles.

Rock was feeling mellow by the end of dinner and, I believed, a bit proud that I had made such a hit with the meal. "Michael and Elizabeth," he said happily, "you haven't tasted anything until you've tried Phyllis's chocolate soufflé. Phyllis, you gotta make 'em your chocolate soufflé."

The Wildings added cheers of assent, and I invited Elizabeth into the kitchen for a cooking lesson. She watched me combine all the ingredients, then we both sat on the kitchen floor while I beat the mixture endlessly. The baking process took an hour, during which I insisted that everyone tiptoe so the soufflé wouldn't fall.

The evening ended at two in the morning amid great feelings of camaraderie. I worried about how Elizabeth and Rock were going to report for work in the morning. As I expected, Rock awoke with a monstrous hangover and threw up a couple of times. I prepared him a Bromo Seltzer and he left woozily for the studio. Nothing, not even a world-class hangover, could prevent Rock from going to work.

SEPTEMBER 30, 1955

An important date, for two reasons. For one, it was the day I moved into Rock's house. Ever since he had bought the place, I had spent several nights a week there. But the Fairfax Avenue apartment was still my home, a symbol, I suppose, of my independence. Rock kept urging me to share the house with him—"It's lonely when you're not here," he said.

My friend from MCA, Ray Stricklyn, had moved to Hollywood for an acting career and needed a place to stay. "I'll sublet my apartment to you," I said.

The decision was made. I was moving my clothes into Rock's house that morning when I heard the telephone ring. Rock answered it. I heard him say a few words and hang up. Then I could hear him sobbing.

Rushing into the living room, I saw his grief-stricken face. I had never seen him so sorrowful before, and it frightened me.

"What's the matter, honey?" I said. "Is it your mother?"

"No. James Dean." He started to cry, and I put my arms around him.

"What happened?" I asked.

"He's dead. Smashed up his Porsche near Salinas."

Now his big frame was convulsing in sobs, and I struggled to hold him. I asked him why the news had shattered him.

"Because I wanted him to die."

"But why would you want anyone to die?"

"Because I hated him. I was jealous of him because I was afraid he was stealing the picture from me. I've been wishing him dead ever since we were in Texas. And now he's gone!"

It was days before Rock overcame his black depression. I tried everything I could to break through to him. I reasoned with him, I argued that he had nothing to blame himself for. It had been an accident, that's all, a brutal accident. Rock couldn't be reached. He was overcome by guilt and shame, almost as though he himself had killed James Dean.

I felt lonely, shut out from his innermost feelings. Frightened, too, because his mood was so unrelenting. What kind of love did we have, anyway, if I was unable to comfort him?

7

An Engagement, Sort Of

ONE MORNING after he had finished his work on *Giant*, Rock stopped by Henry's office. He sat down on the floor in the large entry room and rested his head on one chair and his feet on another. Rock never sat when he could stretch out.

I continued answering the phone and typing letters while Rock just stared at me with his silly, irresistible grin.

"Look what I got for doing a television show," he said, holding up a tiny box.

"That's nice," I said, continuing with the typewriter.

"Come over here and look at it," he said.

"Well, I'm a little busy right now."

"No, I want you to see it."

"Oh, all right."

I walked around the desk to where he was lying. Inside the box was a single white diamond on a white-gold band.

"You like it?" he asked.

"It's nice."

"Put it on."

"I don't want to put it on."

"Put it on!"

So I did.

"You like the way it looks?" he asked.

"It's okay."

"You can have it."

Something in my Minnesota upbringing insisted that it wasn't right to accept such a gift. "I don't want it," I said, handing him the ring. I couldn't understand why he was so persistent. Was he trying to make a tender gesture but wasn't able to manage it?

"You keep it," he insisted.

"No, I don't want it."

"I want you to have it."

We went back and forth like two kids in an argument, until finally I said, "All right, I'll wear it," thinking to myself that I would return it in a few days.

Was it an engagement ring? Rock never said it was. I only wore it with him, and never in public—that would have given the gossip columnists too much to speculate about. If it truly was meant to be an engagement ring, the gesture was typical of Rock: to hand over a ring he had been given on a television show and do it without ceremony and without commitment—while lying on the floor. I was less than thrilled.

DURING THAT AUTUMN of 1955, Rock kept asking me to quit my job at the Willson Agency. I resisted. My work with Henry wasn't going to make me rich, but it was stimulating in an odd sort of way. I enjoyed working with attractive, talented people and helping, if only in a small way, to build their careers. I still had no ambition to be a career woman. But I also had no desire to become mistress and house-keeper for a movie star.

Rock grudgingly accepted my decision to continue working. He delighted in sharing the house with me, disregarding the possible damage to his career. In those days, unmarried couples simply didn't live together. If our living arrangement had been publicized, his popularity with the teenagers, who were the mainstay of his audience, might have plummeted. And their parents would have been shocked. Rock and I made no great secret of the fact that we shared a house, but we didn't broadcast it, either. Fortunately, although we were considered a "hot item" by the columnists, none of them printed how close we were.

Rock and I often spent weekends in Palm Springs. Rock loved the desert because of the clean dry air, the lovely view of the mountains, the peace it offered after the constant demands of Hollywood. I loved it for the same reasons, and for the contentment it bestowed on Rock. A friend of mine, Manuel Alvarez, knew the manager of the Lone Palm Hotel, and he made the reservations for us—I was too shy, because Rock and I weren't married. I had Manuel request the same room, one with a king-size bed. I had found that sleeping with Rock in a normal-size bed was impossible.

We had a marvelous time in the desert, swimming, sunning, going to the movies, shopping at Manuel's store, Prego, a chic men's shop on the grounds of the Desert Inn in the heart of Palm Springs. Sometimes, to avoid the highway traffic on Sunday, we drove back on the scenic Palms-to-Pines road through Idyllwild.

Rock's passion was waterskiing. He was determined to become the perfect skier: "I want to be the best of any of my friends." I sat in the back of the motorboat while the pilot pulled him over the Salton Sea. Over and over again, Rock would get up on the skis, then fall off. The boat would circle around so he could grab the ropes once more and start over. After innumerable crashes into the water, he became more adept. He never tired.

"I couldn't do this in front of anyone else," he told me. "I couldn't bear having them see me looking like a clown. I'm not a bit embarrassed when you see me fall, because you don't make fun of me."

At the Henry Willson Agency, I was assuming more responsibility with the clients. Henry liked to make sure that they were all happy, so I was designated to call on them at work. One day I drove to Universal Studios for lunch with John Smith, who was playing the young male lead with Lee Marvin and Eva Marie Saint on "The General Electric Theatre." John had been my next-door neighbor at the Fairfax apartment. Our bedrooms were back-to-back, and some nights I would have to pound on the wall for quiet when John and a girlfriend were engaging in gymnastics. John and I had an agreement: if he would wash and polish my car, he could borrow it for dates.

In the Universal commissary John introduced me to Ronald Reagan, who was the host of "The General Electric Theatre." He gave me a warm handshake and made me feel he was really glad to meet me. I also met Kathy Adams, who was playing a small role in the show. Kathy and I formed a friendship that has lasted to the present day, through good times and bad. At the time she was dating her future husband, Louis L'Amour, the writer of western novels.

I was always amazed at Henry's instinct for talent. One morning he dropped a magazine on my desk. "Look at this kid," Henry said. "Isn't he good-looking?"

It was a copy of *True Romances*. A boy on the cover was in an embrace with a young girl. "Yes, he's very attractive," I said.

"Call the magazine and find out who he is."

I called *True Romances* and learned the boy's name was Coby Bennett. At least that was the name he was using as a model; his real name was Carmen Orrico. Henry called his mother in Brooklyn.

"This is Henry Willson calling from Los Angeles," he said in his smoothest tones. "I am a motion picture agent. I just saw a photograph of your son on the cover of *True Romances.* How old is he?"

"Sixteen," his mother said.

That gave Henry pause, but he continued: "I'd like to come to New York and meet your son. I think he is very handsome, and I believe I can find him work in the studios. Maybe a contract with one of them."

Mrs. Orrico agreed, and in a few days Henry flew to New York to see the boy. Because of his age, there were problems in bringing him to California, but Henry worked them out. Within three weeks the renamed John Saxon had a contract with Universal and soon became a favorite with teenagers.

When Henry signed Natalie Wood to an agency contract, he didn't realize he was also signing a stage mother of the first order. Mrs. Gurdin had been a ballet dancer, and her daughter became the surrogate for an unfulfilled career. She had already pushed her Natasha into acting at the age of five; now she was striving to bridge the girl's awkward teenage years.

Mrs. Gurdin was a frequent visitor at the office. "Where's Henry?" she demanded.

"He's having lunch at Fox," I said.

"When will he be back?"

"I don't know."

"Tell him to call me as soon as he gets back. I've called him the past two days, and he hasn't returned my calls. I can't get an answer at his house. What's the matter with him? I see in *Hollywood Reporter* that William Wyler is casting a new picture, and Henry hasn't even taken Natalie to see him."

Henry never danced to anyone else's tune. Mrs. Gurdin could call him a dozen times, and he would never respond unless he felt like it. He considered himself omniscient in terms of what was best for his clients. He would listen to their complaints—and he would listen carefully if they were important clients—but in the end Henry made the career decisions. He had total confidence in himself and in his ability to manipulate both his clients and his customers. His principal method: sex.

Behind the façade of the witty bon vivant was a hard-boiled Machiavelli who would do anything to promote his clients' careers. This meant collecting on favors provided for people with positions of power. Years after I left Henry's employ, one of his clients told me that Henry provided beautiful starlets for midnight rendezvous with Howard Hughes. One morning Hughes made an angry phone call to Henry. One of the starlets had brought her mother along.

I learned that Henry was a virtuoso at arranging sexual affairs. Heterosexual, homosexual, bisexual—you name it—he was a master. His machinations were invisible to me at the time I worked for him because he operated in total secrecy. He managed to have his clients, male or female, at the right place at the right time to effect a seemingly casual liaison that would do the clients or Henry some good. I found out that he arranged for producers' wives to be serviced by handsome young studs. If a producer or director preferred boys, he could manage that, too.

What this amounted to was not only pimping, but a form of blackmail as well. Henry was too suave ever to make threats, but I'm sure the information he knew about people in power helped win him favors.

God help the poor client who refused to play Henry's game. I heard more than one of them say, "No, goddammit, I'm not going to do anything so cheap and crummy!" That person was not only dropped from the agency, Henry delivered the classic line: "You'll never work in this town again!"

It was no idle threat. Henry began a campaign of vilification that could ruin the actor's reputation. He could do it in the sliest ways, such as telling a producer, "You wouldn't want him in a western. How about a tutu?" Or, "You may have trouble with the love scenes; he's the biggest fairy in town."

Variations would be: "I hope you don't have the same trouble as on his last picture, when he couldn't remember his lines." Or, "He'd be a pretty good actor—if he could just get over that drinking problem."

I was appalled by Henry's slanderous campaigns, never suspecting that one day I would be one of his targets.

ROCK WAS UNCHARACTERISTICALLY elated about his career in the fall of 1955. Ever since I had known him, he had been totally insecure about himself as an actor. His jealousy of James Dean was evidence of that. He had felt fairly comfortable cranking out the Universal potboilers. He had become less confident as he began working with first-rate directors in important movies. Now he realized that he had done his best work in *Giant*, thanks to George Stevens's careful guidance. Henry Willson kept telling Rock, "You're going to get an Academy nomination for *Giant*, I know you are." Rock shrugged off the notion, but I could tell he savored it.

ONE EVENING in June, I heard a knock at the door. Rock went to answer it, then I heard him shut the door firmly. He took me by the hand and led me to the small bedroom. "Stay here," he instructed. I had never seen him so upset.

He closed the bedroom door, and I heard him striding to the front door. Someone entered, and I heard two voices arguing, Rock's and another man's. I couldn't hear what they were saying, but both were angry. Then I heard footsteps approaching the bedroom.

"You keep looking in this direction; there must be some-one in here," the other man said.

My heart stopped. I slid down behind the bed just as the door opened. Apparently I wasn't seen, because he re-treated. A few minutes later, I heard the front door open and close, then a car raced down the driveway with a screech of tires.

When Rock returned five minutes later, I asked, "Who on earth was that?"

"The creep who was my roommate when I lived in Lau-rel Canyon," Rock said. "He walked up here, so I drove him back to Sunset."

"What did he want?"

"Money."

Rock would say nothing more. I tried to question him, but he refused to discuss the incident. I couldn't imagine why he insisted that I hide from his visitor. Why? What did Rock have to hide? I felt like an actor in a spy movie, but I didn't know the plot. Not until much later did I realize the significance of the visit.

8

Wedding in Santa Barbara

"LET'S GET MARRIED."

We had just ordered dinner at Frascati's when Rock let go the thunderbolt. I couldn't believe he was serious.

"Oh, come on!" I said.

"I mean it. Let's get married."

He *was* serious. I felt as if an electric shock had permeated my body, but a very pleasurable shock. He wants to get married, I said to myself, trying to maintain my composure. This was what I had dreamed about but wouldn't allow myself to hope for. I opened my mouth and nothing came out. I could feel the tears starting to form. Dammit, Phyllis, don't make a fool of yourself! You're supposed to be happy, not sad. I grabbed Rock's hand and peered into his eyes, praying that he realized what he had said.

"I've got it all figured out," Rock said excitedly. "Henry has a friend who has a boat in Nassau."

"You've discussed this with Henry?"

"No, of course not. But he has this friend, see, and we could have the wedding at sea where the reporters wouldn't bother us. It would be so romantic."

"I don't like the idea."

He was crestfallen. "You mean you don't want to get married?"

"No, no. I want to marry you. But not on a boat. Pat Devlin and I have sworn that we will be each other's bridesmaid when we get married."

"We'll bring Pat along."

"No, Rock, I want it to be right. Not on a boat somewhere in the Caribbean. My mother would think I'd gone crazy. I want to be married by a Lutheran minister."

"Oh." Rock was stopped in his tracks. "Well, we'll talk about it tomorrow."

When we announced to Henry that we were going to marry, he welcomed the news. "Don't worry, I'll arrange everything," he said glowingly. And he did.

Everything had to be done with speed because it was early November and Rock had to return November 28 to begin work on another important film, *Written on the Wind*, costarring Lauren Bacall, Robert Stack, and Dorothy Malone.

"You can have the wedding next Wednesday," Henry declared.

"Wednesday! That's only a week from now!" I exclaimed. "I don't have a dress, a going-away outfit."

"Don't worry. Pat can go shopping with you. You can pick out everything you need." His agent's mind was going a mile a minute. "Also, you and Rock can go to Dr. Brandsma for your blood tests. He'll hurry them through, and he'll keep them quiet, too. We've got to move fast and secretly. If the papers get the scent, we'll have a mess on our hands. Rock, don't tell *anybody* at the studio, not anybody. Now I figure the best plan is for you to get the license in Ventura late Wednesday afternoon. Use your own name, Rock, and try to get away before anyone recognizes you. Then you can drive up to Santa Barbara, and we'll have the wedding in a hotel."

"But I want a Lutheran minister," I insisted.

"Yes, dear, you'll get your Lutheran minister," said Henry.

Excited as the mother of a young bride, Henry went off to commence his whirlwind plans. Rock and I gazed at each other delightedly. I had never seen him so elated.

"Pat will be my maid of honor, that's for sure," I said. "Who's going to be your best man?"

"Jim Matteoni," Rock announced.

"Jim Matteoni? Is he in the picture business?"

"Good God, no! He was my buddy from kindergarten all the way through high school. Great guy. I'll call him right now and see if he and Gloria can fly out for the wedding."

Rock placed a call to Evanston, Illinois. I was amazed to hear him talking to Jim. Rock sounded so joyful and inti-mate—it was a side of him I had never seen. Later I thought how unusual it was that he had never mentioned Jim Matteoni to me. Jim had obviously been an important figure in Rock's early years, and yet Rock had never talked about him. But then, Rock never discussed his life before becoming an actor. Never. I wanted to know what he was like when he was a boy. I wanted to know if he had the same kind of happy Midwestern childhood I had known. Or if it was not so happy—as I suspected—I wanted to share that, too. But he wouldn't talk about those things. He seemed bent on eliminating Roy Fitzgerald from his mem-ory. His life began when he became Rock Hudson.

Jim Matteoni was flabbergasted by Rock's news. Jim was a music teacher who had small children, and he said it would be difficult to drop everything and fly to California. Rock was insistent, and Jim said his and his wife's parents lived nearby so maybe they would sit with the children.

Arrangements were made, and the Matteonis were scheduled to arrive on the Tuesday night before the wedding.

Next, Rock placed a call to Pat Devlin. "What are you doing next Wednesday?" he asked her.

"What do you think I'm doing? I'm working," replied Pat, who was now employed at an advertising agency.

"How would you like to go to a wedding? Phyllis's and mine."

Pat was floored. She had known that Rock and I were serious, but she didn't think we were *that* serious. I came on the telephone to confirm the news and told Pat to meet us that evening at Henry's house in Stone Canyon.

Henry was in his glory, rattling off instructions like a general before D Day. Each of us was given directions. We were to carry them out as if nothing unusual was afoot. Above all, secrecy. Tell no one that Rock and I were getting married.

The next morning Rock drove off to the studio for a day's work, though he would take time off for a blood test. I embarked on my own missions, all the things that most brides take months to accomplish. I wanted something special as a gift for Rock, and I found a handsome gold St. Christopher's medal. Appropriate, I thought, since he was commencing the most important journey of his life.

One of my duties was to report for a blood test, which was required for a marriage license in California. Henry sent me to the Beverly Hills office of Dr. Maynard Brandsma; he was Henry's doctor, and Henry sent his clients there, including Rock. I was immediately charmed by Dr. Brandsma, a handsome man with an amazing background. He had been born in Holland and had been practicing as a doctor in the Dutch East Indies when the Germans invaded his native country. He came to California and studied at Stanford University, but was so eager to help his subjugated country that he joined British Intelligence. Later he switched to the American OSS, and his undercover adventures would make a dozen movies. After the war he returned to California, and now he had a Beverly Hills practice with such patients as Humphrey Bogart and David Niven.

After his nurse Mary took the blood sample, Dr. Brandsma brought me into his office for a friendly chat, inviting any question I wanted to ask. After the examination, I saw him conferring seriously with his nurse. At first I thought he had found something wrong with me. But he didn't mention anything like that, and it wasn't until many years later that I discovered the cause of his concern.

I was due at I. Magnin's at three to meet Pat Devlin and pick out my wedding dress. By the time I arrived, Pat had pulled out several dresses for my approval.

When I had started planning, I asked Rock what color he would like me to wear. "Yellow," he said. Pat and I exchanged pained expressions. "Yellow is *not* my color," I said. "How about beige?" "Maybe cocoa brown," said Rock.

I picked a Paris brown peau de soie with a full skirt and a portrait neck. "Rock will love this color," I enthused. Then I realized my mistake in mentioning his name.

The saleslady immediately asked, "Are you marrying Rock Hudson?"

"Rock Hudson?" I laughed, perhaps a little too loudly. "Heavens, no. You must have heard me say Bach. I have a friend named Bach." Both Pat and I laughed hilariously, and the saleslady apparently wrote it off as bridal hysteria.

On Tuesday evening, Rock and I drove to Los Angeles International Airport to meet Jim and Gloria Matteoni. Rock was overjoyed to see them, and I liked them immediately. They were down-to-earth people, like the ones I used to know back home. We took them back to Rock's house and settled them in the guest bedroom. Rock and Jim laughed over old times until far into the night, and Gloria and I talked about weddings and things.

Henry Willson had been busy too. He ordered the wedding cake from his favorite bakery. He made arrangements for Rock and me to honeymoon in Jamaica, and he reserved space on a flight from Los Angeles to Miami at one-ten on Thursday morning. He made the reservations in the name of Mrs. and Mrs. Charles Roy. "If Mrs. Roy is leaving the country, we'll need to know her first name," the clerk said. Somehow Henry came up with the name of Pearl. Ever afterward he called us Charlie and Pearl.

Henry drove to Santa Barbara on Tuesday night and managed to assemble the whole production for the wedding day. He reserved a bungalow at the Biltmore Hotel. He found a florist and ordered long-stemmed roses and gladiolas to be placed in wicker baskets. My bridal bouquet was white carnations, white sweetheart roses, and gardenias. Not my favorite flowers, but then Henry never bothered to ask.

Next, Henry looked in the telephone book for Lutheran churches. He found the Trinity Lutheran Church and called the Reverend Nordahl B. Thorpe. "Could you come to the Biltmore this evening and marry a couple from Los Angeles?" Henry asked. "The groom's name is Fitzgerald." The minister said he could.

Henry telephoned Pat Devlin because he knew she would be the only one who had her wits about her. He instructed her to pick up the wedding cake and get all of us organized so we could reach Ventura before the license bureau closed. Henry would meet the Los Angeles contingent at a motel a block from the bureau at four in the afternoon.

When I woke up on my wedding day, November 9, 1955, my mind started dancing. I couldn't believe that this was really happening to me, that Phyllis Gates of Montevideo, Minnesota, was marrying Rock Hudson, the movie star. So many things to do. I had to get the health certificate at Dr. Brandsma's office, have my hair combed out, try on the dress and make sure it was hemmed properly. Rock and Jim Matteoni drove off to the studio for the morning. Among her other duties, Pat picked up the ring Rock and I had chosen on Tuesday—a beautiful platinum band with baguette diamonds.

For all his efficiency, Henry forgot one thing: a photographer. When he telephoned the house to report that all was in readiness, I told him, "I want photographs of my wedding." Rock didn't seem to care, but I insisted.

We weren't going to tell anyone about the wedding, not even our parents. Security had to be tight or the press would find out and ruin our plans. Jim and Gloria Matteoni had been sworn to secrecy. The only one Rock alerted was Jack Diamond, head of publicity at Universal, so he would be able to release the news after the wedding.

That afternoon at the house was bedlam. I was trying to get all my wedding clothes together while packing for Jamaica. Rock was doing the same, without much luck.

By the time Pat arrived at three with the cake and the ring, we were in complete disarray. "Come on, guys," she urged, "we've got to be at the license bureau before five!" We managed to get the clothes and the cake in the trunk of Rock's Buick convertible. He drove, Pat and I sat in the front seat with him, and Jim and Gloria took the rear.

"Have you got the ring, Jim?" Rock asked over and over again, and Jim kept assuring him.

"We're never going to make it in time," Rock fretted as he sped northward on Pacific Coast Highway. I insisted we were going to make it, and then my heart sank when I heard a siren behind us.

A motorcycle policeman had passed us going in the other direction, and Rock figured he was safe. But the officer turned around and chased us around several curves until Rock had to stop.

"But, officer, we're trying to reach the Ventura courthouse before it closes," said Rock. "We're getting married tonight." He held his breath, hoping the policeman wouldn't recognize him.

The policeman had no sympathy for the situation, nor did he appear to recognize Rock. "Well, buddy, if you keep going this way you'll arrive in a hearse," he said, taking out his pad. The ten-minute delay frayed everyone's nerves further.

Finally we arrived in Ventura, found Henry, and rushed into the license bureau.

"My name is Roy Fitzgerald," Rock announced solemnly. That's the way he signed the license, and the woman clerk gave no indication that she knew his movie name.

"By the way, is this license good in any county?" Rock asked. She assured him it was. "That's good," he said, "because we may get married in Monterey." Rock had been coached by Henry to say that. Henry figured that if news of the license did leak out, reporters would be scurrying all over Monterey trying to find the wedding.

We arrived at the Biltmore at six. The bungalow had two bedrooms, so Pat and I dressed in one, and Rock and Jim dressed in the other.

Reverend Thorpe hadn't known he was going to marry a movie star. He only knew that we wanted a brief ceremony, not the usual Lutheran wedding, which is quite long. He began with a little sermon based on Joshua 24:15— "As for me and my house, we will serve the Lord."

"You can be happy together if you follow these sacred words," he said. I'm sure he said some wonderful things, but I didn't hear them. I felt as if I were floating far overhead, gazing down at my own wedding.

"Stand still!" Pat whispered as she noticed my wavering. My face was flushed, and I wondered if I was going to faint. Fortunately, Pat linked her arm in mine and steadied me.

"Do you take this man to be your lawfully wedded husband . . ." I heard the words, and I knew I was supposed to respond. I managed to croak a weak "I do."

"Do you take this woman to be your lawfully wedded wife . . ." Rock answered with a resounding "I do!" The vows were the brief ones of most Protestant services—

without the word "obey." Neither Rock nor I liked the connotation.

Rock placed the ring on my finger. He didn't want a double-ring ceremony, saying that he'd just have to keep removing a ring for movie roles.

Rock gave me a long kiss, and it was all over in fifteen minutes. Reverend Thorpe shook our hands and wished us great happiness. I learned later that he had grown up in Willmar, Minnesota, only fifty miles from my hometown.

Henry and Jim kissed me, and Gloria and Pat kissed Rock. I suddenly remembered my family. "I've got to call my mother and tell her the news," I said.

"Oh, no," instructed Henry, "you've got to call Hedda and Louella first. They'll still have time to make the home editions."

Henry sat Rock and me down on the beds and coached us in what to say to Louella Parsons and Hedda Hopper so the columnists could print the news in the morning papers. Henry also called Jack Diamond, head of publicity at Universal, so he could release the story to the wire services and other media. Then I was allowed to call my family.

Mother and Dad had already gone to bed when I called. Mother was floored. She had known, of course, that I had been dating Rock. She certainly didn't know that I had been living with him—the news might have killed her—or that we were even close to getting married. But she gave us her blessing, as did my father. Rock called his mother and invited her and Joe to meet us for champagne when we returned.

The six of us drove to dinner at the Talk of the Town restaurant, where there were many toasts and much merrymaking. Then back to the bungalow. While Rock and I loaded our clothes and the flowers into the car, our friends showered us with rice. Henry had provided a three-pound bag for ammunition. I tossed the bridal bouquet to Pat, of course, since she was the only unmarried woman there. I knew that she was wishing her own wedding would come soon.

Kay and Joe Olsen were waiting for us when we returned to Sparrow Lane. Rock carried me over the threshold, then kissed his mother, who was a bit miffed because she hadn't been invited to the wedding. But she understood when Rock explained that we had to maintain complete secrecy or the whole plan would have been ruined.

More toasts, more champagne, and my head was reeling. How I wanted simply to fall in bed instead of climbing on a plane and flying all night to Florida. But the joy of the occasion kept me going, and Rock and I alternated between spurts of laughter and tears.

Jimmy Matteoni drove us to the airport. Rock and I sat in the back seat, arm in arm, and he teased me: "How does it feel to be an old married woman?" "Now you have to be nice to me because I said 'I do.'" He loved to stare at my wedding band.

The plane left at midnight, and Rock put his arm around me while I nestled on his shoulder. He smiled at me. "Well, Bunting, we did it."

"Yes, darling, we did." I had never been so happy. Rock and I had quite a long courtship and now we were married. I couldn't believe it. Life was beautiful.

9

Honeymoon in Jamaica and Manhattan

WE HAD TAKEN A TAXI from the Miami airport to the Saxony Hotel, where we discovered that the Henry Willson planning service had broken down.

"Sorry, we have no reservation in the name of Mr. and Mrs. Charles Roy," the desk clerk said. "We're really booked because we have a Coca-Cola convention in the hotel. But I can give you a small room on the eighth floor."

"We'll take it," said Rock, who was weary from the all-night flight.

When the bellboy showed us into the room, I was aghast. It looked like an oversized closet.

"Rock, we can't stay here," I said.

"It's okay by me," Rock replied.

"But it's our honeymoon! Look at this room. No view. It's tiny. Let's go downstairs and ask for something better."

"No, they'll recognize me."

"Then *I'll* go."

The desk clerk listened to my plea that we had just been married in California and needed a better room. He responded immediately with an ocean-view suite. I suspect that he now realized who the honeymooners were. The wedding story was being featured in every newspaper in the country.

Rock and I embraced on the balcony, watching a red globe of fire rise out of the Atlantic. We glanced at the bed and decided what we needed most was sleep, not love. "Later," we agreed, almost in unison.

We awoke at four in the afternoon—it was one o'clock, Pacific time—and decided to see the sights of Miami. Rock rented a Cadillac convertible, and although we received some knowing looks from the hotel employees, Rock's identity did not seem generally known. We toured down Collins Avenue, and I pointed out some of the sights I had visited when I was an airline stewardess.

"I know the most wonderful place for stone crab," I said. "It's called the Lighthouse. You'll just love it."

At the Lighthouse we ordered the crab and a bottle of Pouilly-Fuissé, and I was overcome with happiness. Rock seemed the same way. We laughed at everything. When the waitress said, "May I take your order?" we screamed with laughter. She must have thought we were drunk. We weren't. We just felt as if we had left this planet.

Midway through dinner, Rock looked at me in a peculiar way. He raised his wineglass and said, "I toast you, my Bunting. We must always stick together and not let anyone try to pull us apart." His face turned suddenly sad. "You know, Hollywood is full of a lot of vicious people who spread stories and rumors. You must never believe any of them."

He looked on the brink of tears, and I had never been so touched by anything he had said.

"Here's to us," he continued. "I love you."

"I love you, too," I said, barely able to speak the words because I was so choked up.

When we returned to the Saxony, reporters were lying in wait. They were very polite, and Rock answered all their questions. "Now, if you don't mind, gentlemen, I'd like to be alone with my wife on my honeymoon," he said.

From the balcony we could see the ocean waves, luminescent in the hotel floodlights, rolling gently toward the beach—not the crashing breakers I had come to know in California. The November air was amazingly balmy, just like summer. We watched the view for minutes, locked in each other's arms. Then we went to bed and made passionate love. The best ever, not brief and hurried, as it had often been. I drifted into deep sleep knowing in my heart that I had never been so happy in my life.

MONTEGO BAY stretched below like an aquamarine jewel. Rock and I stared out the plane window in wonderment at the sheer beauty of the sight—the narrow white beaches fringed with cocoa palms, the clean wood-frame buildings, the verdant hills climbing up from the sea. What a dreamy place for a honeymoon.

Happily, there were no reporters at the airport, as there had been in Miami when we left. We were greeted by a functionary of the Jamaica Tourist Board, who assured us that everything would be done to guarantee our pleasure and privacy. A car from the Half Moon Hotel took us to register—finally as Mr. and Mrs. Rock Hudson. We were escorted to our bungalow, white and immaculate, a few feet from the gentle Caribbean.

"I'm hungry," Rock announced. It was not an uncommon condition for him. I was hungry too, though I wasn't sure which time zone my stomach was in. We walked up to the hotel for lunch.

The dining room was open-air on a wide terrace overlooking the bay. Three long tables offered an eye-filling display—salads of shrimp, lobster, tuna, chicken, each in a conch shell; hot dishes, cold dishes, every kind of tropical fruit, bananas, pineapple, papaya, mango, plus some I'd never seen before. A steel band was playing Jamaican music. Rock ordered a bottle of wine, and we plunged into the buffet.

"I'm stuffed," he said afterward. "We've got to watch our waistlines. I'm going to start another picture as soon as we go back, and they won't want me looking like Sydney Greenstreet."

"Let's split a dessert," I suggested. Each of us had half a banana tart with our coffee.

We needed some exercise to work off the lunch. Back at the cottage, we put on our bathing suits and took an hour's walk on the beach, picking up driftwood, examining shells, skipping rocks along the water. We talked about everything and nothing.

During the afternoon we sat on the beach in front of our cottage, having rubbed each other with lotion—we had been warned about the Caribbean sun. We cooled off in the ocean, though the water was almost as hot as the air. We played gin rummy and took a nap. When we awoke, it was time for dinner.

Dinner at the Half Moon Hotel was fairly dressy, so Rock wore a jacket. Another sumptuous meal, interspersed with dancing. I felt full of warmth and love. Since we'd married, Rock was more open with his emotions. During dinner he leaned over and whispered in my ear, "I love you." He was more caring than he had ever been.

We met a charming couple from New York, Joan and George Axelrod. At first the name didn't register, then George said, "I wrote a play called *Will Success Spoil Rock Hunter?*"

"Oh, *you're* the guy!" Rock said. "Why didn't you call it *Rock Hudson?*"

"I wanted to, but my lawyer wouldn't let me. He thought

you might sue. So I combined your name and Tab Hunter's."

Rock and I both said we wanted to see the play, which was a big hit in New York.

"Then you've got to come there before you go back to California," George said. "Here's another reason: Moss Hart is tossing a big party next week, and I know he'd love to have you come. I'll call him tomorrow."

Rock and I looked at each other with the same expression of "Why not?"

When we returned to the cottage, Rock said, "I'm stuffed again. Let's take a swim. Make us sleep better."

"You go ahead, I'll watch."

I sat on the beach chair and watched while he plunged into the water and swam far out into the bay, so far that I worried that he might get a cramp after eating. When he stepped out of the water, I marveled at the beautiful human specimen I had married. The broad shoulders, the slim hips, the perfect proportions. No wonder the teenagers swooned over him.

Rock toweled off and looked down at me with that irresistible grin. "Wanna play?" he asked. It was his standard invitation to lovemaking.

"What—right here?"

"Right here."

We made love in the sand with even more passion than Deborah Kerr and Burt Lancaster in *From Here to Eternity.*

WE RELAXED the following day, swimming a bit, sunning a lot, and napping to get adjusted to the new time zone. Then we decided to do some Jamaica adventuring. Rock rented a noisy Morris Minor that was so small he had to ride with the top down. His head was about a foot above the windshield. We had fun taking movies of each other driving from the right side, a novelty for me, but Rock had done it in Ireland. I still have the movies—how young and silly and deliriously happy we looked.

"I've got a friend, Tony Marsella, who lives in Ocho Rios," Rock said. "Let's drive down there."

The hotel packed a lunch for us, and we set off down the narrow black road to Ocho Rios. We had been advised to stop at a rain forest along the way, and we arrived there at lunchtime. I had never seen anything so beautiful. It looked like a scene from an Esther Williams movie, deep-green ferns and vines shading a foaming white stream that cascaded over giant rocks. We sat on a broad flat rock and ate our lunch and drank the carafe of wine, overwhelmed by the magnificence of the setting. Afterward Rock clambered over the landscape to shoot dozens of views with his movie camera.

Tony Marsella and his wife were enormously hospitable, so much so that we stayed all weekend. They had a beautiful house with many servants, and they invited friends to meet us. Rock did a lot of snorkeling in front of their house, exploring the gardens of coral. When we left Tony presented me with an antique silver piece, a mug called a slush bucket that was used to contain coffee grounds. It still sits in my bookcase.

When we arrived back at the Half Moon, the hotel people welcomed us like long-lost friends. "We've made you a little surprise," said the social director. "We understand that tomorrow is Mr. Hudson's birthday. And so we've planned a little party. Tomorrow night at eight, on the patio. Casual dress."

Oh, dear. Rock and I looked at each other with pained smiles. On the way back to the bungalow, Rock said, "I'm sorry, honey, I just wanted to spend my birthday with you. Now I suppose we've got to be nice to all the local dignitaries."

"That's all right, dear," I said. "We've already had more privacy than we could have hoped for. Besides, we have the rest of our lives to be together."

At least we could spend part of Rock's birthday alone on the beach. In the afternoon we visited the open-air market, which was full of beautiful fabrics, sports clothes, handicrafts and other tempting things to buy. I bought some Irish-made tablecloth napkins, a sterling tea strainer, and a pants-and-blouse outfit in white cotton with bright red crabs printed on it.

We dressed rather formally for dinner, despite the instructions of casual wear; we figured it would be expected of a visiting movie star and his bride. We arrived at the patio shortly after eight to find—no guests.

"My God, are they fashionably late in Jamaica?" Rock said. "Maybe we can disappear before they arrive."

"No, that wouldn't be polite after all their planning," I said. "We'll just have to wait."

A waiter came to take our drink orders, and I said, "Thanks, but we'll wait for the others."

"Others?" he said. "There are no others, madame. The party is for you and Mr. Hudson only."

Rock smiled broadly, and we sat down to a delicious meal of Rock Cornish hen stuffed with wild rice, served with great attention and ample white French wine. A calypso band played romantic music, then gathered around the table to sing "Happy Birthday" when the cake arrived, blazing with thirty candles.

Afterward I said to Rock, "That's funny."

"What's funny?" he asked.

"I thought you were the guy who told everybody you wouldn't get married until you were thirty."

"Oh that! Every interviewer asked me when I was going to get married. So I started telling them 'not until I'm thirty' just to shut them up."

"Well, you only missed by eight days."

I awoke the next morning with the residual glow from the birthday party and the lovemaking of the night before. The other side of the bed was empty but still warm and fragrant with the strong male smell that I loved. I heard the shower running and Rock humming.

I opened the bathroom door and felt the onrush of steam. Behind the translucent shower door I could see Rock's tall frame under the spray. Meticulously he was lathering every part of his body, first his arms, then his legs, his shoulders, his chest, his stomach. It was unbelievably erotic. I let my nightgown fall to the floor, and I opened the shower door and stepped inside.

Rock saw me and jumped out of the shower immediately. "I'm finished," he announced in his childlike manner. I was puzzled by his instinctive reaction. Also hurt. I had felt I was doing something innocently sensual, such as any wife might do on her honeymoon. Yet Rock had rejected the gesture, and I didn't know why.

He was sullen for the rest of the day. When I suggested that we go shopping, he said, "Bunting, I just want to be alone." That didn't bother me too much; I enjoyed my aloneness, too. Rock took long walks on the beach, smoking one cigarette after another. There was no way I could get through to him. I had known these black moods before, when he would spend a day in stony silence, his face clouded in gloom. But I never expected it to happen on my honeymoon.

By dinnertime his mood had brightened, and we talked excitedly about flying to New York in the morning. Later I thought to myself, Is this the way it's going to be, Phyllis? Will you be able to tolerate those periods when Rock shuts you out of his life? The answer: Yes, you will have to. Perhaps your love can help him conquer those times of depression. Perhaps not. But your love for him is so deep that maybe you can learn to withstand his dark moods and rejoice when they are over.

JOAN AXELROD carried her fur coat onto the plane. George had his overcoat over his arm. Rock and I came aboard dressed for the tropics. We had had no thought of going to New York on our honeymoon and had brought no cold-weather clothes.

What a sight we were, walking down Fifth Avenue in our resort clothes and tennis shoes, with only raincoats to protect us from the November chill. Passersby stared at us, thinking we were a couple of nuts. Then, when they saw Rock's face, they looked in disbelief. I could almost hear them saying, "No, it couldn't be!"

Rock was totally oblivious; he could have been anywhere. Then he saw Saks Fifth Avenue, and he steered me into the store. We bought street clothes for the New York autumn and party clothes for the Moss Hart affair.

The clothes were sent to the hotel, and we continued our stroll on Fifth Avenue. "Let's go in here," Rock said when we reached Tiffany's.

The sight of Rock Hudson in the store stirred the staff into activity. Rock led me to one of the counters. "Let's see what they have to offer," he said.

Trying not to appear eager, the salesman brought forth a number of jeweled settings. "Like this?" Rock asked. "It's nice," I said. "Like this?" "It's nice." Finally a pin with a large blue sapphire surrounded by tiny diamonds was placed on the velvet pad. "Oh, that's beautiful!" I sighed.

"We'll take it," Rock said.

The gorgeous pin was packed into a tiny box and handed to Rock. Outside the store he placed it in my hand and said, "Happy anniversary. It's two weeks today. Do you want to try for a thousand?" He kissed me on the cheek, and we continued walking up the avenue. I put my hand inside the pocket of his raincoat. People may have continued staring at us, but I didn't notice. My eyes were too full of tears.

Rock was never so tender as during those few days in New York. Once I overheard him say to George Axelrod, "You know, Phyllis is a wonderful girl; she could charm the birds right out of the trees." More than once he told me,

"You know, if you ever decided to become an actress, Phyllis, I'd have to move over. You'd be a big hit."

He enjoyed having our photograph taken when we attended the play *Will Success Spoil Rock Hunter?* We laughed throughout, drawing special enjoyment since we had become friends with the playwright. Afterward Rock told George, "I'm really mad at you for not calling it *Will Success Spoil Rock Hudson?* I always wanted to have my name in lights on Broadway, and this may be the only chance I will have had."

The Moss Hart party was smashing, as expected. Rock got a special thrill out of introducing me to his celebrity friends as his bride, and there were lots of kisses and congratulations. The guest list was loaded with famous people from Broadway and Hollywood, from Truman Capote, Bennett Cerf, Tennessee Williams, Beatrice Lillie, and Oscar Hammerstein II to Kirk Douglas, Henry Fonda, Yul Brynner, Anne Baxter, and Claudette Colbert.

I saw a familiar face staring at me from the other side of the dance floor. Marlon Brando. I felt a momentary thrill. Did he remember our brief encounter three years before? Apparently not. He walked over to my table and said, "You have the whitest teeth I have ever seen in my life." I thought Brando's remark about my teeth was funny and I started to laugh. He gave me a kiss on the cheek and walked away.

I was dazzled by the guests at the Hart party. I had attended stellar gatherings with Rock in Hollywood, but this one was different. These people were talking about books, plays, politics, not the incessant "picture talk" you hear in Hollywood. I enjoyed myself immensely. I especially enjoyed having Rock sit across the crowded table and wink at me whenever no one was looking. I had a Cinderella-like feeling of regretting that the ball—and the honeymoon—would soon be over and we would be returning to Rock's all-absorbing career in Hollywood.

We were both exhausted when we arrived at LAX.

Henry greeted us outside the gate, and he seemed very full of himself. When we drove to the top of our driveway, I noticed something different in the garage. My red Ford convertible was gone. Sitting next to Rock's car was a shiny new black Ford convertible with a Continental kit and a huge red ribbon wrapped around it.

"My God, I can't believe it!" I squealed. "Is that for me?"

"Yes," Rock said delightedly. "I had Henry turn in your car while we were away. That's why I had to call the office so often."

"So—the two of you were in cahoots!" I exclaimed.

"Do you object?" Henry asked.

"Of course not!" I said.

10

Newlyweds

ROCK BEGAN *Written on the Wind* immediately after we returned from our honeymoon. That was fine with me; Rock was always happiest when he was working. He was even more enthusiastic about filming after the *Giant* experience. Observing the creative methods of George Stevens had been an inspiration to Rock. "I want to be a director," he said, and I tried to encourage his ambition. I thought it was wonderful that he was expanding his horizon beyond acting. At night we talked for hours about how he could break into directing, what kind of films he would like to make, what actors he would enjoy working with.

We newlyweds were being feted in different ways. Rock's mother gave me a shower with her friends in Pasadena, and I received many practical things for the kitchen and the linen closet. Rock's grandmother sent me a beautiful handmade quilt from Illinois. The Universal executives entertained Rock and me at a welcome-home luncheon at the studio. I was the lone woman at a long table with all the top brass.

Al Zugsmith, who was producing *Written on the Wind*, tossed a cocktail party in honor of Mr. and Mrs. Rock Hudson and Yvonne de Carlo and Bob Morgan, also newlyweds. I decided to take Ray Stricklyn along. Ray was trying to get a foothold as an actor in Hollywood, and I thought it would be advantageous for him to meet some of the power figures.

Ray was agog at the wall-to-wall celebrities. I was impressed too, by the turnout and the warm hugs and kisses from people I had seen only on movie screens. Rock seemed to glow as he was congratulated over and over again. "Yeah, she's great, isn't she?" he said when people complimented me.

"Where've you been keeping this lovely girl, Rock?" Hedda Hopper demanded. "You know, she's much prettier than she photographs." It was a compliment I cherished. I had rarely been pleased with the photos taken of me, whereas he seemed incapable of being photographed badly.

Rock's costars in *Written on the Wind* were there—Robert Stack, Dorothy Malone, Lauren Bacall. Humphrey Bogart dropped in from work. He gave me a big kiss and growled to Rock, "This dame's too good for you, kid." I liked Bogie immediately.

The byplay between Bogie and Bacall was right in character. "I'm going home," he announced.

"Since when did you ever leave a party as long as the booze was flowing?" she asked.

"Since a young wife made me an old man. I got an early call. Are you coming with me or aren't you?"

"I'm staying. Rock'll give me a ride home, won't you, Rock?"

"Sure," Rock said.

Bogie gave me another kiss and departed.

Rock and I stood together throughout the party, as if in a receiving line. Everyone pressed forward to greet us. After the congratulations, the talk, of course, was about the picture business.

When the party started to thin out, Rock decided it was time to leave. Four of us piled into Rock's convertible, Betty Bogart and Ray Stricklyn in the back seat, Rock and I in the front. We were all in high spirits as we drove westward on Sunset Boulevard, unaware of the chilly November air. When we arrived in Holmby Hills, Betty acted as a ribald tour guide, pointing out the houses of her neighbors: "Over there is the home of Judy Garland and Sid Luft; at this hour they're on round four of their nightly boxing match." When we arrived at the Bogart house, she announced, "And here we are at the home of that talented pair, Humphrey Bogart and Lauren Bacall, and their two adorable children, Leslie and Stephen. And to all a good night."

IT WASN'T ALL PARTY for Rock and me. He was working every day on *Written on the Wind,* a very dramatic movie, and he liked to come home at night, pour himself a drink of Scotch and collapse. He enjoyed lying on the couch with his head in my lap. Then he would talk about the events of the day, often with scathing remarks about his fellow performers. This actor always walked sideways. That actress kept blowing her lines.

Rock liked my cooking. I knew what he enjoyed: meat and potatoes and gravy, hearty food like his mother used to cook. But when I noticed a roll developing around his midriff, I cut back to steaks and vegetables.

After dinner Rock often grinned, "Wanna play?"

Sex with Rock was always passionate; he knew all the right moves. But it was usually brief. I didn't complain. I realized that all husbands were different and perhaps he was just going through a phase when he couldn't control his exuberance. I believed we would be married a long time, and Rock would learn to please me as well as himself. Meanwhile it was great while it lasted.

When he went to sleep, Rock always liked to have his arm over me. Nice for him, not for me. I believe he was really six feet six, not six feet four, as his studio biography claimed. His arm weighed a lot. Going to sleep with that big weight on me was not easy, and I tried to wiggle out from under without disturbing him. If he did wake, he lifted his arm back on top of me and murmured, " 'Night, Bunting."

Hotter than ever with the fan magazines, Rock was inundated with requests for interviews in the wake of our marriage. As always, he fulfilled them all. I now became an integral part of Rock's publicity, with certain limitations. The Sparrow house was often the subject of "home layouts," which meant that a photographer would shoot us in the house and outside, trying to simulate our normal activities. So Rock and I would seem to be watching our new color television set, a gift from his appearance on "I Love Lucy." Rock and I would pose in the kitchen while I was supposedly whipping up an omelet. I would watch while Rock purportedly was barbecuing a steak. They had us do everything but pose in bed, and Rock, slave of the media that he was, might have consented if the photographer had asked.

We did layouts away from the house, too. Once we were joined by George Nader and his date, Mara Corday, for a picnic in the desert that was titled "Hollywood Exposé . . . Hollywood a crazy, mixed-up town? Peopled by oddballs and weirdies? Let's take a look at four typical citizens . . . Sorry to disillusion you."

And so we posed getting out of Rock's car, carrying picnic baskets, clambering over fallen trees, eating the picnic, snoozing under the palms.

"There's a good reason why George Nader and Rock

Hudson have become such fast friends and it's a wonderfully simple one. In a madhouse town, where battiness is practically a vogue, these two guys are terrifically, sensationally, supercolossally normal. That makes them the odd ones. After all, when everybody else is talking about his psychiatrist, his divorce, or his love affairs, these two haven't a thing to say. George is a happy bachelor, dating pretty girls and never losing his heart or his head to a one . . . Rock, after a good deal of pressure from his publicity advisers to take out glamour girls and maybe marry one, found himself a swell, nonprofessional gal early in his Hollywood career. The publicity men ranted, raved and threatened, but Rock steadfastly dated his Phyllis, courting her for two years just like any boy back home. Then he married the girl and has been perfectly happy ever since . . ."

In all of the fan magazine layouts and stories, I was the silent partner.

"Don't talk to the press," Rock instructed me. "Oh, if Hedda or Louella or Sheilah comes up to you at a party, be polite, but don't say anything. Talk about the weather or clothes or anything. But don't give them anything they can quote."

I never did. I followed my husband's instructions, and I didn't give any interviews. Of course that didn't stop some reporters from appearing to quote me. But whatever they printed was either secondhand or totally fabricated.

It amazed—and often appalled—me to see my personal life reported in such intimate detail, sometimes accurately, usually not. Is there any other profession in which the leading figures are subjected to such scrutiny? Movie stars must be the only ones. Most of the ones I've known accepted that as one of the necessary adjuncts to their careers. Some even enjoyed it. I think Rock did. He never complained about prying interviewers, never fretted about critical items or bad reviews. He loved playing the role of Rock Hudson, both on-screen and off. He liked that much better than being Roy Fitzgerald.

I was constantly amazed at how fan magazine writers could invent endless variations on the same theme. For instance, this article from *Movie Life:*

WHAT PHYLLIS FOUND OUT ABOUT ROCK

Unlike some Hollywood wives whose names we won't mention, Mrs. Rock Hudson didn't marry the man and then dedicate her life to trying to change him. Wise beyond her years and equally anxious to live in harmony and peace, the former Phyllis Gates made every effort to know Rock as a friend before she came to live with him as his wife. Anything but eloquent when he discusses himself in general and his marriage in particular, Rock sums up the situation thus:

"Phyllis is the best thing that ever happened in my life. She not only understands actors and their work, most important of all, she understands—*me!*"

A hypersensitive man of simple tastes, marriage to the wrong girl could have ruined Rock's life. However it is no lucky accident that Phyllis is the right girl for him. She herself made every effort to make sure she was right, and the thing that impressed her the least about Rock Hudson was the fact that he *was* Rock Hudson.

The thing that impressed her most?

"Rock never ceases to amaze me," she confided to a friend recently. "I've worked with actors, and they love being who they are—twenty-four hours a day. Rock loves his work, but I think he'd be the happiest man in the world if he could just take some sort of magic pill and turn into someone else when he's away from the camera! He's the most unspoiled, unselfish, and unself-centered man I have ever met. Believe me, I could never have married him if he wasn't. After all, an actor is just a husband when he comes home from work, as far as I'm concerned. My husband is special because he's a very special human being—and *not* because he is Rock Hudson!"

Etc., etc., etc.

Rock's mother even got into the act with an article somebody wrote for her that appeared in *Movie Mirror*:

WHAT MARRIAGE HAS DONE TO MY SON
By Kay Olsen

. . . Phyllis is a good cook in her own right, so good, in fact, that she has to watch my son's diet or he'll gain weight like crazy.

She knows Rock's number one weakness, which is desserts. And not just chocolate soufflé. He loves pumpkin pie, strawberry shortcake, napoleons, in fact, just about everything that's rich in calories. To keep him from eating too much of it, she lets him fill up on steaks, salads, chops, and other nonfattening foods, till he hardly misses the desserts, which she serves about once a week.

Phyllis's influence on my son has been good, subtle, and probably more apparent to me, because I know him so well, than it would be to an outsider.

For instance, in the old days, he no sooner got home than he slipped into dungarees. Dress shirts, ties, jackets were out of the question. Yet I don't recall recently seeing Rock in dungarees.

He's become neater and better organized. As a boy he never picked up his clothes, and after a few years I gave up even trying to make him do it. It was easier to do it for him.

It wasn't all sweetness and light. One day I passed a magazine stand, and I saw a blazing headline: DOES PHYLLIS BOSS ROCK? After much hemming and hawing, the author came to the conclusion that I didn't. But still, I was upset by the headline, and I complained to Rock about it. "Oh, don't read those things," he said lightly. "They're all bullshit."

THE FIRST MONTHS of our marriage were filled with first-time events. For our first Thanksgiving, I wanted to entertain Rock's mother and her husband for a feast of my own making. I planned the menu with great care, interpolating some of the dishes my mother made back home. Everything went well until I discovered that the housekeeper hadn't turned on the oven. She was a day worker who had been employed by Rock before I moved in, and I always felt a sense of resentment of me as an interloper in her domain. Whether or not she tried to sabotage my Thanksgiving dinner I'll never know, but she caused an embarrassing two-hour delay in serving the turkey.

My own thirtieth birthday fell on December 7, 1955. (Rock and I were born only nineteen days apart, even though news stories of our wedding listed me as anywhere from twenty-four to twenty-seven. The studio may have wanted for me to seem younger, but I have never lied about my age.)

"Where do you want to go on your birthday?" Rock asked.

"L'Escoffier," I said immediately. The restaurant atop the Beverly Hilton was my favorite, since it was there that I fell in love with Rock.

The evening at L'Escoffier was almost as dreamy as the one we had spent a year before. Superb food, marvelous wine, romantic music. I could have danced until dawn, but Rock kept looking at his watch. "I think it's time to go home," he said.

"But why?" I asked. "You don't have a call tomorrow."

"Yes, but I'm a little pooped. Besides, you want to get a little lovin' on your birthday, don't you?"

"Let's go."

I snuggled close to Rock all the way home. When we drove up the driveway, I noticed he was glancing all around. After we walked in the house, he seemed terribly upset. Then I noticed some figures outside the patio window. It gave me a start until I noticed who they were.

"Oh, my God!" Rock exclaimed. "I forgot to leave the back door unlocked."

He opened the door for a dozen people who poured into the house shouting "Surprise!" and "Happy birthday!"

They had been standing out in the cold night air, waiting for us to return.

The surprise party was a Henry Willson production, done with his impeccable taste. A waiter brought in a tasty buffet, a bartender started serving drinks. Rock put Harry Belafonte records on the hi-fi, and soon everyone forgot the cold outside. All of our close friends were there: Pat and her boyfriend Rux; George Nader; Mark Miller; John Smith, Ray Stricklyn, Steve Evans, and their dates; Henry with a couple of his handsome new clients.

At one point in the evening, Rock disappeared, then came back with a box tied with a red bow. He carried it very carefully, piquing my interest over what could be inside. I untied the bow, peered inside the box, and saw two dark eyes staring out at me. It was a tiny gray poodle.

"Oh, he's darling!" I exclaimed, cuddling him to my cheek. "Rock, sweetheart, you know how much I love dogs!"

Rock was glowing with pride. He told me how he had gone to a kennel near Universal Studios the day before and had picked out the puppy. He took it to Pat's apartment for her to keep overnight and bring to the surprise party.

"Well, what are you going to call him?" Rock asked.

I studied the adorable little dog. "He's so small," I said, "I think I'll call him Demitasse."

THEN CAME our first Christmas as husband and wife. Rock loved Christmas. He made it a big celebration. He bought a huge tree for the living room and spent hours decorating it. On his days off from *Written on the Wind*, he went shopping with Pat Devlin, who helped him with my sizes and my taste in clothes. Pat and I were recently reminiscing about the fun she and Rock had shopping together. Pat said, "Everywhere we went, we were overwhelmed with salespeople. Rock drew so much attention that it was no wonder he was catered to when we appeared in one exquisite boutique after the other. He bought a gorgeous fur stole, some beautiful jewelry, sweaters, slacks, skirts, dresses—you name it and Rock bought it. I tried everything on for him as you and I were about the same size. It was so much fun watching him select one gift after another and hearing him say, 'Will Phyllis like this?' or 'This would be perfect for her' or 'This is Phyllis's favorite color.' What fun he had spoiling you with his love and generosity. We had a marvelous time, and to this day I have always thought of Rock as your special Santa—he did love you so."

Of course the big gift from Rock to me that Christmas was the mink stole. He was cute about it, planting a decoy package under the bed to put me off the scent. But then I read an item in one of the gossip columns.

"What's this about your buying me a mink stole for Christmas?" I asked.

Rock was crestfallen. "What kind of a son of a bitch would print an item like that and spoil the surprise?" he said angrily.

I tried to make up for it by oohing and aahing over the mink. I didn't have to act. It was a gorgeous stole, the most luxurious thing I had ever owned. Rock seemed very pleased as I paraded in it around the living room.

My big gift to him couldn't be a surprise, either. It was a baby grand piano which I had had finished in "gunsmoke" to match the decor of the house. It was his first piano, and he loved to tinkle out tunes. He was a pretty good player.

Before we opened the gifts on Christmas morning, Rock and I had a special project to do. Several weeks earlier, while we were watching television, a newscaster was commenting on all the needy families in the Los Angeles area. We wrote to the station and got the names of some of those families. Then Rock and I made up a list of all the foods necessary for a holiday dinner: turkey, potatoes, vegetables, milk, cranberries, etc. I telephoned Jurgenson's and asked them to make up fifteen identical boxes containing these items. When Christmas morning arrived, Rock rented a station wagon and off we went to deliver the boxes. Rock carried them into the houses and I explained to the families that this was a Christmas present from us. In one home there were three small children and the refrigerator was empty except for a carton of milk. We felt *wonderful* when we returned home.

Later that morning we opened our presents to each other. Rock had wrapped all of mine at night in the storeroom. He gave me blouses and skirts and nightgowns, and I gave him sweaters and slacks and socks and—a pair of cuff links.

The cuff links had a story. Rock and I used to love attending the openings at the Coconut Grove of performers like Lena Horne and Harry Belafonte. Most of all, we enjoyed dancing to Freddy Martin's romantic music. Our favorite number was "Tonight We Love," based on Tchaikovsky's Piano Concerto No. 1. So on one gold cuff link I had engraved "Tonight," on the other, "We Love."

When Rock read the inscription, he looked at me curiously. As sometimes happens, he drifted off into a territory where I couldn't reach him. I didn't understand. Had he somehow misread the message of the inscription? I had expected that he would be charmed by the gift. But he remained indifferent. Why? I was confused—we had a wonderful life and were very much in love. Could it be that I just imagined he was indifferent? I don't know. I loved Rock so much that I think I overlooked a lot of things.

The entire living room was strewn with presents. Besides our own gifts, Rock received dozens of packages from people at the studio. Mostly liquor, cases of aged Scotch and fine French wines. We never had to refill our liquor supply all year.

I wanted to have Christmas dinner alone with Rock, and I cooked a goose with all the trimmings from a recipe in the *Gourmet* cookbook. That evening we were invited to the traditional Christmas night party at the Bogarts'.

Their Holmby Hills house was blazing with Christmas

lights, and just about all of Hollywood's elite were there. Betty was a gracious hostess, making sure that everyone knew each other and had plenty to eat and drink. Young Leslie and Stephen made a brief appearance in their night-clothes, then were taken off to bed by their nanny.

Bogie adopted me. I think he perceived that I was a country girl among all the sophisticates, and he liked my naïveté. Every time he saw me across the room, he made a funny face at me. He grabbed me by the arm and led me to the bar, saying, "C'mon, let's have a drink. I was *born* one drink behind."

We passed Spencer Tracy and Katharine Hepburn, who were sitting in a corner. "You know, Spence, you never really made it," Bogie muttered. "There was always Gable." Tracy smiled sourly.

Around midnight the entertainment began. Everyone sat down on couches, chairs, or the floor as Judy Garland went to the piano with her accompanist, Roger Edens. For half an hour she belted out "The Trolley Song," "Liza," "Over the Rainbow," then Frank Sinatra took over. June Allyson and Peter Lawford sang a duet, and Noël Coward did "Mad Dogs and Englishmen." The million-dollar show went on and on, and I was totally enthralled.

I thought I must be dreaming. Most of the guests I had seen on stage or in the movies, and here I was in the middle of them! I was so excited, and I whispered to Rock, "I want to meet *everyone.*" "Okay, honey," he said. He took my hand and we started to walk around so I could meet some of the other stars. Everyone was dressed so beautifully, and I was thrilled to be there. Bogie was a perfect host, always on the move, introducing people, getting conversations started. Two or three times he came over to me and asked, "Can I get you anything, Phyllis?" He was such a kind, thoughtful man.

When Rock and I finally said good night, Bogie gave me an extra hug. How happy he seemed, so proud of Betty and his two children, so pleased to be surrounded by all his good friends of the movie business. Almost exactly a year later, Rock and I visited his house again. It was in the afternoon, when he received his visitors. Too weak from cancer to come down the stairs, he was lowered in the dumbwaiter, then wheeled into the living room to exchange banter with his friends. He was frail and weak as he sipped his martini, but he was still able to toss out light-hearted insults. Two days later he was dead.

No loss had affected me so deeply. Bogie had been my friend, my ally and protector. He had singled me out because, I believed, he liked me and he realized that I was somewhat lost in the Hollywood whirl. He was a dear man, totally unlike his screen image. I'll always remember him with great fondness.

11

Movie Star's Wife

"LET'S DRIVE TO ACAPULCO!" Rock proposed in January. He had finished *Written on the Wind*, and Universal had given him two weeks' vacation before starting *Battle Hymn*. It sounded like an adventure, so I agreed.

We packed our summer clothes and embarked early one morning, crossing the border at Mexicali by noon. Then the adventure began. Gone were the smooth highways of California. The Mexican roads were unpredictable, to say the least. You never knew when you were going to hit a big hole or ford a stream or wait until a herd of sheep passed by. The Buick bounced and jounced and bolted and shuddered until my spine began to complain. It didn't bother Rock at all. He sat happily behind the wheel, singing the few words of Mexican songs he could think of.

We had expected immediate summer the minute we

crossed the border. Wrong. The nights were achingly cold, and Rock and I had to snuggle closely to keep warm. Fortunately we found nice little hotels along the route, including some that overlooked the Gulf of California. Both Rock and I loved Mexican food, and we found many family-style places with great food.

Every day we drove for miles on end, encountering no one except an occasional farmer and his burro. Nothing to look at but cactus. I was terrified that we might blow a tire or break an axle, but luck was with us. We had good times in Mazatlán and Guadalajara, poking around in the shops and bazaars for fabrics and silver.

After five days of hard driving, we finally reached Acapulco, and what a lovely sight it was. Rock made no reservations, trusting that his status as a movie star would provide entrance anywhere. He was absolutely right. Teddy Stauffer, who was well known by the Hollywood crowd and had once been married to Hedy Lamarr, found us a room at the Villa Vera. Teddy, who had been a principal figure in making Acapulco a world-class resort, took us to La Perla to see the amazing dives by the Mexican boys who soared off the cliff into the rocky lagoon. It was frightening to watch those boys dive off the towering cliff. They had to time their dives perfectly with the rhythm of the waves—and they seemed just inches from the cliff on the way down.

Teddy introduced us to Barron and Marilyn Hilton, who were also staying at the hotel, and to Miguel Alemán, the playboy son of the Mexican President.

Miguel took the Hudsons and the Hiltons to a small private island for a day of swimming and exploring. Miguel and Rock went skin diving while the Hiltons and I watched. Alone on the tropical island, we felt like Robinson Crusoe—except that Miguel had provided a huge basket of food and wine.

The next day a letter was delivered to our hotel room. It was from the captain of a U.S. Navy cruiser who had learned we were in town: "The officers and crew would be honored if you would join us for lunch on board . . ."

"You wanna go?" Rock asked.

"Sure," I said. "It sounds like fun."

We were instructed to report to a certain dock at 1100 hours. There we climbed into a launch and rode across the bay to the cruiser, which loomed larger and larger as we approached. It was like a floating hotel, and we must have toured every part of it, up ladders and down ladders and into the engine room. Rock got a big charge out of being escorted by the captain and sitting down to lunch in the officers' quarters. A different scene from his years as a gob. I enjoyed the admiring looks and occasional whistles from the sailors, and I think Rock was pleased that his wife attracted such a reaction.

Next on the agenda: bullfights and deep-sea fishing.

The bullfights I could have missed. The spectacle was impressive, but taunting and killing a magnificent animal for the cheers of the crowd is not my idea of fun in the afternoon. Rock loved it, though. He thought it was terrific theater, and he shot endless movie footage of every phase of the bullfight.

Sailfishing appealed to me more. At least the odds are more even in that contest. What a thrill to feel that huge weight at the end of your line. What a challenge to keep reeling it in until your fingers are raw and numb. Both Rock and I caught big sailfish. Of course they had to back up the boat to land mine; I could never have landed it by myself. Even so, my arms ached!

"Mine's bigger than yours," I challenged.

"Oh, no, it isn't!" he insisted.

When the two fish were loaded onto the dock and hung for weighing and photographing, mine was longer and heavier. "I told you so," I said kiddingly. Rock was not amused. He seemed perturbed that a woman—his own wife—had bested him in a physical contest. He pouted for a couple of hours, and I decided not to mention the matter again.

Several Hollywood people were staying at the Villa Vera, and we had company for dinner every night. During the day we went sight-seeing or shopping—I bought twenty wedding shirts for friends. The Villa Vera needed our room, so we moved to another hotel, one with a huge garden and dozens of large, brightly colored parrots.

One night we dined with friends at a restaurant with a large mariachi band. In the middle of dinner, Rock excused himself and left the table. Strange, I thought. He didn't usually need to go to the bathroom during dinner. When he didn't return after twenty minutes, I decided to go looking for him.

The men's room attendant said Rock wasn't inside. I looked in the bar. Not there. Finally I walked outside the restaurant, and there I found him. He was hanging onto a lamppost and retching miserably. I explained to the other dinner guests, and I hailed a taxi to take Rock back to the hotel.

The hotel doctor diagnosed it as an acute case of the turista and prescribed some medicine. For two days Rock remained in bed as I did everything possible to relieve his misery. It was my first experience of taking care of a sick husband, and I was greatly concerned.

"There's no way that you can drive home," I said. "I'll hire someone to drive the car back, and we'll fly." I think both of us were relieved not to face that five-day drive again.

ONCE AGAIN we were invited to have dinner with Elizabeth Taylor and Michael Wilding at their home. Again we were greeted by Michael, who seemed somewhat restrained. He explained that he was under sedation for a back ailment.

Michael introduced us to the two other guests, Montgomery Clift and another actor, Kevin McCarthy. Clift lived up to his reputation: he was brooding and sullen. McCarthy seemed bright and intelligent. He kept the conversation alive, meanwhile eyeing Monty to make sure he didn't consume too many drinks.

After half an hour, Elizabeth made her appearance, resplendent in a white gown, laden with jewels. She greeted Rock and me warmly and then turned her attention to Monty. She sat close to him on a couch, and they conversed almost in whispers. According to rumors, they had been lovers while making *A Place in the Sun*, though he was said to be homosexual. Now they were near the end of filming *Raintree County* together. Elizabeth did most of the talking (I learned later that Monty had not wanted to come to dinner, but she had convinced him with several phone calls).

The sedated Michael reclined on another couch, oblivious of the intimacy between Elizabeth and Monty. That left Kevin, Rock, and me to maintain a conversation, which we somehow managed. The dinner was no improvement, though Elizabeth tried to keep things cheerful. It was an uphill struggle, given Michael's sedation and Monty's moodiness.

Shortly after dinner, Monty announced he was leaving. "I think I'll follow you down the hill," said McCarthy, who was worried about Clift's capacity to drive.

The rest of us were settling down to brandy when the telephone rang. A look of horror came over Elizabeth's face. "I'll be right there," she gasped.

"It's Monty!" she told us. "He crashed his car at the bottom of the hill. Kevin doesn't know whether he's dead or alive."

Elizabeth, Michael, Rock, and I rushed to the courtyard and climbed into a car. We sped down the hill to where Monty's car had smashed into a telephone pole. It had collapsed like a broken toy. A few people had come out of their homes to view the accident, and we found Kevin McCarthy among them.

He explained that Monty had been following *him* down the hill, his car coming frighteningly close. Then Monty's car began to weave, and he crashed. "I called an ambulance," Kevin said. "He's inside, but he's in terrible shape."

Without hesitating, Elizabeth ran to the car and struggled with the front door. It was jammed shut, so she opened the back door, climbed over the seat and sat next to Monty's crumpled body. His face, so handsome minutes before, was now a pulpy mask. Elizabeth held his head in her lap, stroking his hair and talking soothingly. Then she was startled by a blinding flash. She looked up and saw a camera pointed at her.

"Get that damn camera out of here!" she screamed.

Rock and Michael were transfixed by the horror of the scene and she yelled at them, "Can't you two help me?" Rock and Michael came to life and they positioned themselves between Elizabeth and the photographer, not allowing him to pass.

I joined Elizabeth in the car and tried to stop the bleeding on Monty's nose and mouth with tissue. The steering wheel appeared to have pushed in his face. I could see that he had lost some of his front teeth. Elizabeth and I stayed with him until the ambulance arrived, then we rode in the front seat to Cedars of Lebanon Hospital.

Elizabeth was composed until Monty was taken into the operating room. Then she became hysterical, and I comforted her as best I could. Later we learned that Monty had suffered a crushed jaw and sinus cavity, broken nose, severe concussion, two lost teeth, and severe facial lacerations. By 7 A.M. his condition was stable, and I took a taxi home.

Rock was angry with me that day. "Why did you go to the hospital?" he demanded.

"I was trying to be of some help," I explained. "Besides, I think Elizabeth needed to have someone with her."

My explanation didn't satisfy him. He asked, "You didn't talk to the press, did you?"

"Yes," I admitted. "Reporters came to the hospital. Both Elizabeth and I answered their questions."

"Never talk to the press!" He stormed out of the house and slammed the door.

Rock didn't talk to me for days. I was puzzled by his attitude. I thought I had acted selflessly, trying to be of help in a drastic situation. But he acted as if I had been guilty of some transgression. Was it because *I* had been in the spotlight and he hadn't? I couldn't find the answer.

ROCK'S NEXT FILM was *Battle Hymn,* a change of pace for him. He was playing the real-life role of Dean Hess, an Ohio minister who had accidentally bombed a German church as a pilot in World War II, killing thirty-seven children. Hess had volunteered for the Korean War, and he organized an airlift to remove orphans from the combat zone.

Rock was excited about working in a movie with combat scenes. "I love war," he told me.

I couldn't believe what I was hearing. "What do you mean—you 'love war'?"

"I do. I think it's exciting."

"Exciting? What about all the soldiers who get killed and mangled? What about all the women at home who lose their sons and husbands and sweethearts?"

"Oh, I don't think about that. I just love war." A strange look came over his face, one that I was to recognize every time I challenged his beliefs. I realized later what was happening in his mind. He was a movie star. Everyone listened to his every word. Magazine writers and columnists recorded his statements and released them for the world to read. At the studio nobody dared contradict him, no one in publicity, makeup, wardrobe, not even the director or studio executives.

But here was his own wife reminding him when he spoke nonsense. I couldn't help it. All my life I had been known for speaking my mind. I had thought that was one of the things Rock found attractive in me during our courtship. Maybe he didn't find it so appealing in a wife.

Otherwise, we had few conflicts in those early months of our marriage. Our social calendar was full. Bob and Rosemary Stack invited us to Palm Springs one weekend. They had a charming Spanish-style house with a large courtyard, and they drove us all over Palm Springs to show us places Bob had known as a boy. We dined with the Stacks at the "in" Mexican restaurant of that time, feasting on nachos and listening to the mariachi band. Rock, fortunately, had forgotten all his bad memories of Mexico.

As we drove back to L.A. on Sunday night, Rock was in a glowing mood. He commented on how much he liked Bob and Rosemary. "You know," he added, "I love the desert. We oughta buy a house down here."

"I'd love it," I agreed. But we never did, and it was twenty years before I moved to Palm Springs, alone.

The Stacks invited us to an informal dinner party at their house on St. Pierre Road in Bel Air. I was introduced to John Wayne, who said, "So this is the bride!" He leaned down and kissed me on the cheek, adding, "May you have many wonderful years together." He was an impressive man, strong yet sensitive, and although he was opinionated, he listened to what others said. I never got the impression he was trying to force his views on me. Duke was wearing cowboy boots, and I thought how marvelous it was that he should always wear them.

Bob Stack showed me his den, which was filled with trophies he had won for his marksmanship. I mentioned hunting for pheasant with my father in Minnesota, and we had a nice chat. I enjoyed talking to several of the guests before Rock arrived—he had been working late on *Battle Hymn*.

Rock didn't want me to talk too much at parties. Maybe

he thought I would embarrass him by not knowing much about show business. Once at a party I saw a group that included Rocky Cooper, Gary's wife. I had admired her style and elegance and I mentioned to Rock that I would like to meet her. "Don't go over there," he snapped. "They'll cut you to ribbons."

Yet Rock enjoyed entering a party with me on his arm. Whether it was because he was becoming a major star or because he now had a wife to bring, Rock had started getting invitations to the most exclusive parties. He had been on the fringe before, now it was fashionable to invite Rock Hudson and his bride to join the cream of Hollywood society. These were the Old Hollywood who entertained each other in their Beverly Hills and Bel Air homes. They were all there at a party Rock and I attended at the home of Clifton Webb and his mother Maybelle: Jack and Mary Benny, George Burns and Gracie Allen, Claudette Colbert and Joel Pressman, Irene Dunne and Francis Griffin, the Cary Grants, the Greg Pecks, the Bogarts, et al.

Naturally I couldn't compete as a hostess on that scale. But I sometimes entertained two or three couples at our house, cooking some kind of gourmet dish. Michael Wilding and Elizabeth Taylor came to dinner a few times, and it was always a hazard with Michael. While Rock and Elizabeth were gabbing in the living room, Michael joined me in the kitchen and whispered in my ear, "You know, Phyllis, I wish I had met somebody like you; you're the person I should have married." He gave me a pat on the behind for emphasis.

"Michael, are you out of your mind?" I whispered. "You're married to the most beautiful, the most talented, the nicest woman in the world. Now don't play games."

I was surprised by the number of passes directed at me, even at the best parties and usually by married men. I didn't know how serious they were, because I never took them seriously. "Why, I'm a happily married woman," I said.

I guess I shouldn't have been too surprised when Elizabeth called a few weeks later to say, "I've got to find someplace to hide. I'm leaving Michael, and the press are going to start hounding me. Can I stay at your place?" And so while reporters were searching all over town for Elizabeth Taylor, she was spending the weekend at our house, sleeping in the guest bedroom.

Grace Kelly became an immediate friend. Rock and I had attended a banquet at which he and Grace were presented a magazine's award as the most popular stars in America. After the program, Grace said to us: "You live up on the bird streets, don't you? I'm renting Gaylord Hauser's house up there. Why don't you come by for a nightcap?"

She served us drinks, and she and I got into a deep conversation about astrology. She was a real believer, and she pointed out that Prince Ranier of Monaco, whom she had met while filming *To Catch a Thief*, had a sign that was totally compatible with hers. At that time rumors were being printed everywhere that she was going to marry the prince and quit her career. She and I continued talking while Rock snoozed on the couch. We were still going at 2 A.M. when she opened the refrigerator and served us some cold chicken.

When Grace married Prince Ranier a few months later, I sent a telegram of congratulations from Rock and me. She sent a handwritten letter of thanks and added, "Please come and play with us!"

Our social life wasn't limited to Rock's Hollywood friends. We also spent a lot of time with Pat Devlin and her boyfriend Rux. Rux invited Rock to help crew his sailboat one weekend, and Rock fell in love with sailing. A few years later he bought his own sailboat.

When Kathy Adams and Louis L'Amour married in 1956, they asked Rock and me to stand up for them. I had to decline for us, because Rock would be gone on location. Rock and I spent many evenings with Kathy and Lou after their marriage, and Rock loved to hear Lou spin yarns of the Old West.

IT WAS IMPORTANT to Rock that his wife make a good appearance. Once he took me to Amelia Grey's and bought me three thousand dollars' worth of dresses, including two beautiful black Trigères. I needed an extensive wardrobe because of all the social events we had to attend. It was great fun for me, and it seemed comforting to Rock that I accompanied him. He became more and more at ease, especially when I coached him—ever so subliminally—about some of the social graces. I reminded him to compliment the hostess at parties and to hand out tips in restaurants so the staff wouldn't say he was a cheapskate. He was surprised when I wrote a thank-you note every time we were entertained. He had never thought of doing it himself.

"I depend on you too much," he once told me. "You don't know how much I listen to you."

I was startled by his admission. All I could think of to say was: "Isn't that what marriage is all about?"

12

Rock Hudson Close Up

ROCK SPENT FOUR WEEKS in Nogales, Arizona, filming the war scenes for *Battle Hymn*. He didn't invite me to visit him, and I didn't ask to go. Again I realized he didn't want me around while he was working.

When he returned from Nogales, our usual life resumed, usual being a round of premieres and parties. But there were quiet moments, too. Rock still liked to come home from the studio, mix a drink, and put his head in my lap. That was his idea of domestic bliss. Those were the times when he talked about his work, and it disturbed me that he was more and more critical of those he dealt with. Little things bothered him—a director's caustic remark, an imagined snub in the commissary.

"Honey, you can't let those things bother you," I told him. "You're King of Universal right now. Enjoy it."

There were things about his career that bothered *me*. He never read his contracts. He just signed them, assuming that Henry Willson would make sure they were okay. He never read scripts, leaving that to Henry too. MGM sent a script for a remake of *Ben-Hur*, seeking Rock to play the leading role.

"I can't read that script—look how big it is," Rock said.

"I'll read it," I said. Afterward I told Rock, "Please do this picture; it's a wonderful story."

Henry vetoed *Ben-Hur*: "I don't want Rock in costumes —he'll look foolish." And of course, Charlton Heston won the Oscar for it.

OTHER THINGS bothered me about Rock. Why was he constantly chewing his nails and picking at his fingers until they were raw and bleeding?

His mother had often complained that Rock had been messy as a boy. He hadn't changed. At night he stepped out of his clothes and left them on the floor. In the morning he put them on again. I was forever picking up after him, just like his mother. Nor was he very clean. He would go for two days without a shower, and revel in it. Like an impish little boy, he'd hold up his arms and say, "Wanna smell my pits?" I would tell him, "Rock, for God's sake, take a shower! Stop acting like a child!"

Nor did he like to brush his teeth. He thought it was boring. I kept telling him he had film on his teeth. When I mentioned that they would photograph yellow in Technicolor, he brushed them.

When I asked him to empty his ashtrays, he responded, "People like dirty ashtrays. It makes them feel at home."

Rock gave me one hundred dollars a week to take care of all my expenses. There was no way I could pay for hairdressing, the maid, laundry, dry cleaning, food, clothing, etc., on one hundred dollars a week. Fortunately, the accountant at Henry Willson's office—Henry handled all of

Rock's expenses, including utility bills—provided charge accounts at the department stores as well as Jurgenson's, the gourmet grocery store.

One evening Rock and I watched a World Series game on television while drinking one of our favorite vintages of wine. As the game progressed, we chose sides. "I'll bet you a million dollars my team wins," Rock announced.

"You're on!" I replied. My team won and Rock dutifully wrote a check for one million dollars. Sober in the morning, he hunted desperately for the check, found it, and tore it in shreds.

UNLIKE MOST OF THE PEOPLE I met in Hollywood, Rock didn't gossip. He had no interest in the latest scandal or who was doing what to whom. He sometimes made acidic remarks about his fellow workers, especially Tony Curtis. Rock and Tony had arrived at Universal at the same time. Both had been given the star buildup, and they were rivals for the same roles. Although they were outwardly friendly, Rock disparaged Tony, referring to him by his real name, Bernie Schwarz. I think Rock was jealous because Tony was so self-assured and outgoing, which Rock was not.

Rock really could be quite shy. One morning we were having rolls and coffee in the Beverly Hills Hotel coffee shop. Across the room was Elvis Presley, whose music Rock greatly admired. Rock and Elvis noticed each other at the same time, but all Rock could manage was a weak "Hello." He was too shy to tell Elvis how much he liked the Presley style.

The boyish quality that movie fans admired in Rock on the screen was for real. When I first knew him, Rock often went down the hill to visit the Weirs, who lived at the bottom of his driveway. Don and Betts had five children, and their freezer was filled with several flavors of ice cream. Rock liked to sit in the kitchen and talk with Don and Betts and some of their kids while eating ice cream. He could consume a quart at one sitting.

ROCK HAD UTTERLY NO INTEREST in politics. I never knew whether he was a Republican or a Democrat, or neither. About politicians he said, "They're all crooks." I don't think he ever voted.

He never read books. I bought popular novels, thinking I might be able to get him interested. I suggested he might even find a project that he could direct or produce. He didn't care. He was too nervous to read. He worked crossword puzzles instead.

Rock had a beautiful body, but he did little to keep it that way. I couldn't get him interested in golf or other sports. His one physical activity was gardening. He could spend hours on the slope behind our house, pulling weeds and planting flowers. His only other hobby was editing film. He loved to sit over his editing machine in the back room, running our vacation movies and splicing them into some kind of order.

He liked to go to the theater when we visited New York, but we rarely saw plays in Los Angeles. Rock was always too tired, and he didn't want to fall asleep in public.

Rock was a heavy smoker. Maybe three packs a day, although I didn't count. He seldom drank excessively. He enjoyed a Scotch or two before dinner, and he loved wine, as I did. Once I told Ed Muhl, the Universal production chief, how much I liked wine. The next day he sent fifteen cases of wine to the house, including some fine German and French vintages.

Rock fancied himself a gourmet cook, and one day he announced, "I'm going to make a special dinner for you and George and Mark and Pat. I want you out of the house. I'm going to do everything."

It sounded fine to me. Pat and I went out to lunch, and we spent the afternoon shopping. When I arrived home, the place had been transformed. Balloons everywhere. Bouquets of flowers. The round marble table was meticulously set with our best china and silver, place cards on each plate. Little dishes of peanuts and mints were in the living room. Rock served each course with great ceremony, and all of us praised his wizardry in the kitchen.

"Oh, Rock, what a marvelous meal!" I enthused. "I'm going to let you cook every night." I changed my mind when it took me two whole days to clean up the kitchen!

In nearly every interview Rock gave about our marriage, the question of having a family arose. Rock always answered that, yes, he would like to have a family, but we wanted to wait a couple of years. He talked about his future children: "We want them to be relaxed, have fun, know how much we love them—and make up their own minds about their lives."

Those articles amazed me. Rock and I never seriously discussed having children, but sometimes as a joke he would say, "I'd like to have ten kids." I laughed and replied, "Not with me you don't." I practiced birth control with a diaphragm, figuring that when the time came, we would have children. Naturally I wanted to have a family, like my brothers and sisters. But at thirty, Rock and I were still fairly young. We still had some living to do, some adjustments to make, before taking on the responsibility of parenthood.

Rock wasn't the least bit religious, even though he had attended church as a boy. Whenever I referred to my Lutheran upbringing he scoffed. "The Bible? It's a bunch of fairy tales."

MY SEX LIFE WITH ROCK was far from satisfactory. He knew all the steps to arouse a woman's passion, but he could not contain his own. He employed means to prevent it, such as stopping for a brief period, but still he reached his climax before I desired. Like many wives, I tried to be understanding and sympathetic, telling him, "That's all right, honey." But I was never very good at acting, and eventually my frustrations came to the surface.

"Can't we try again?" I pleaded after a maddeningly brief encounter.

"One doesn't want hors d'oeuvres after eating dinner," he replied.

"You're talking about dinner for one!" I exclaimed.

Finally I persuaded Rock to consult Dr. Brandsma about his premature ejaculation. Dr. Brandsma said Rock's problem was probably due to anxiety and would go away in time. In the meantime, he prescribed a salve which would make Rock less sensitive. It proved to be fairly effective, and our lovemaking was more satisfactory—for me, at least.

From his proficiency in the early stages of the love act, I gathered that Rock had ample experience—and certainly as a movie star and an extremely attractive man, he would have had plenty of opportunity. But he certainly had some strange ideas. "All women are dirty," he once told me. "Their private parts remind me of cows." I was flabbergasted. What an unloving thing to say. Thereafter, whenever he issued the invitation "Wanna play?" I went to the shower and scrubbed and scrubbed before going to bed.

In many ways, he was a male chauvinist. He wanted me to cook his meals, take care of the house, be available for sex when it pleased him, accompany him in public without being vocal. "Don't talk to the press, don't talk to anyone," he instructed me. I didn't know whether he was being protective or jealous. There was a strain of jealousy in his nature, and he liked to know where I was at all times. Despite the number of passes I received from people we met, he never had any grounds for suspicion.

One morning I stepped out of the shower and felt the floor tremble. Earthquake! That was one part of California living I could never get used to. Then I realized the shaking wasn't in the pattern of an earthquake. It was something else. I opened the bathroom door and heard dance music coming from the living room, along with repeated thumpings. I looked inside and there was Rock leaping around the room. He was completely nude, his genitals tucked between his legs.

"What are you doing?" I said.

He looked up, somewhat embarrassed but not overly so. "I'm a ballet dancer," he announced.

I couldn't help laughing at such a comical sight, this big hunk of a man leaping about like one of those dancing hippos in *Fantasia*. Later I thought it was more weird than funny.

Rock and I cutting our wedding cake.

(UNIVERSAL)

The wedding party: Jim and Gloria Matteoni, Reverend Thorpe, bridegroom and bride, Pat Devlin, Henry Willson.

Henry placed calls to Hedda and Louella
immediately after the ceremony.

Henry delighted in pouring rice down my bosom;
Rock was convulsed.

(GERRY MURISON)

Sipping a tropical drink on the beach at Jamaica.

(GERRY MURISON)

Portrait of a happy bridegroom.

(UNIVERSAL)

The Universal brass gave Rock and me a luncheon on our return to Hollywood.

Rock giving me a piggyback ride.

(JOHN BRYSON)

The Hudsons at home.

Rock and Demi sitting on his Buick.

My mother, Rock's mother, and me at
Henry Willson's party.

(SOTELO)

Rock was a trifle upset because my sailfish
was slightly bigger than his.

(UNIVERSAL)

Rock seemed to have that faraway look
when I visited him on the set of *Written on
the Wind*, and met Lauren Bacall
and Robert Stack.

(VAN WILLIAMS)

In the lobby at the Roxy with Jayne
Meadows and Chill Wills for the premiere
of *Giant*.

We respond to a joke at a dinner for
George Stevens.

13

Clash in Rome

EVER SINCE I LEFT HOME, I have visited my family in Minnesota each summer, without fail. My return in 1956 was a special one, because I would be introducing my famous husband to my family and friends. Minnesota would be the first stop in what would be a fabulous trip.

With *Giant* still unreleased and being touted as a major film, Rock was inundated with offers. Universal couldn't prepare enough films to keep him busy, so the studio decided to take advantage of the huge amounts it was offered for loanouts. A deal was made with MGM for Rock to costar with Sidney Poitier and Dana Wynter in *Something of Value*, based on the Robert Ruark bestseller about the Mau Mau uprising in Kenya. The movie was to be shot in some of the same areas where the violence took place.

Perhaps as consolation for profiting from Rock's services,

Universal offered us a two-week, all-expenses-paid holiday in Europe. Naturally I was thrilled. What a way to see Europe for the first time. Rock was also enthusiastic. The studio was providing a car and driver to escort us through Italy, and Rock loved Italy.

"First I've got to visit my folks," I told Rock. "Why don't I go to Montevideo first, then you fly to Minneapolis and pick up a car. You can drive over to meet my family, then we'll fly to New York and Europe."

I left the last week in June and spent some time with Mother and Dad, eating her fine cooking and getting acquainted with my nephews and nieces.

Rock arrived five days later, and he charmed my mother and father. After dinner on his first night in Montevideo, we were sitting in the living room and having a nice chat when some kids arrived at the door asking for Rock's autograph. Like any news in a small town, word had spread of Rock's arrival, and the youngsters naturally wanted to see a movie star. Rock was gracious for the first ones, but then he became irritable. I was afraid he was going to have a temper tantrum in front of my family. Oh, dear, I thought. Sometimes Rock acts like a spoiled child, like now, without showing any concern for my parents' or the kids' feelings.

I took Rock in the kitchen and said to him in a quiet voice, "Rock—"

"I'm not going to sign any autographs!" he announced.

"Rock, please be kind," I pleaded. "This is a small town, just like the one you grew up in. Having Rock Hudson in town is the biggest thing that has happened since the last tornado. My parents know all these kids' parents. So just be nice to them and they'll go away."

He changed his whole attitude and the kids departed happily. Mother and Dad were impressed, and I think they were convinced that their daughter had made a wise choice.

That night we went to bed in my old room upstairs. It was one of those hot, humid summer nights, and I was miserable. The same double bed was in my room, and Rock occupied most of it. As always, he insisted on keeping his arm around me.

"Rock, it's too hot," I said. "I can't sleep like this."

"But I've got to hug you, Bunting," he insisted. "I can't sleep unless I know you're there."

"Rock, I've got to go to the other bedroom."

"Don't leave me, honey. Stay with me."

I couldn't resist that kind of entreaty. But as soon as he slipped into a sound sleep, I wiggled out from under his arm and carried my pillow to the spare bedroom.

My sister Marvis gave a dinner party. Rock spent most of the time in the den, playing with her two children, Janet and Steve. He was very friendly and open with them, and I thought what a good father he would be. After dinner we all gathered around the piano, and Rock played while we all sang.

My other sister, Verna, also had a dinner party, and Rock amused her children, Arlen and Linda. He seemed totally at ease and was often hugging my family, and they hugged him back. "Are you going to fix me some mashed potatoes tonight?" he asked Mother. He insisted that Mother and Dad would have to fly out to California and visit us, and they did, the following January.

After my coaching, Rock tolerated the neighbor kids who came around to ask for his autograph. He even seemed pleased that our local Hollywood Theater dug up one of his old pictures, *Back to God's Country,* and scheduled it with an ad: "CONGRATULATIONS, ROCK HUDSON! Montevideo joins in wishing Phyllis and you every happiness! The Hollywood is very happy to present one of your finest motion pictures for all to see and enjoy."

The Montevideo *News* covered the story:

News that a celebrity was in Montevideo over the weekend spread like wildfire among the younger element of the town's citizenry and had quite a few adults talking excitedly, too.

The celebrity was, of course, handsome movie actor Rock Hudson, whose wife (the former Phyllis Gates) has been visiting with her parents, Mr. and Mrs. Leo Gates, here for the past week.

A Father's Day picnic had been planned by Mr. and Mrs. Gates in honor of their daughter on Sunday, so Rock's arrival made the gathering of the immediate family complete.

On Saturday evening Hudson showed films of the couple's honeymoon trip to Jamaica and also of their trip to Mexico. Members of the family took pictures of the celebrated couple on Sunday.

Mrs. Gates reports that two youngsters recognized Rock as he was getting into a car here Sunday and word of his presence spread rapidly. By early afternoon the Gates lawn was covered with a crowd of young people who stood expectantly in a drizzling rain, clutching pencils and pieces of paper, waiting for an autograph. The Universal star was kept busy for a time as he signed his name again and again.

Hudson made a very good impression on his new family. Mrs. Gates said that despite the fact that he is a celebrity, he is a "down to earth boy" and she "adores" him . . .

I think Rock enjoyed the visit to Montevideo. On the drive to Minneapolis he said how much he liked meeting my family and how Montevideo reminded him of his hometown of Winnetka. We spent a couple of days in Minneapolis and drove all around, stopping for a canoe ride on Lake Calhoun. Our hotel was the Raddison, which was right next door to the Dayton department store. I couldn't resist taking Rock up to the third floor to see if any of my friends still worked in the sportswear department. I found two old friends, and I said, "Oh, this is my husband." When they looked up and saw who he was, they nearly swooned.

I don't know what my friends at Dayton's were thinking, but they were certainly surprised when we came by to say hello. They must have known I had married Rock, as there was lots of press about it. Yet they both turned beet red when they saw him! Rock was holding my hand and I felt very proud of him. He seemed pleased to meet my friends, and I thought how handsome and darling he was.

New York was the first stop in our fabulous journey. *My Fair Lady* was the hottest ticket on Broadway, and Universal managed to do the impossible and get us seats on the aisle. Both Rock and I were entranced as we watched Julie Andrews and Rex Harrison in their roles as Eliza Doolittle and Henry Higgins.

Edna Ferber invited us to dinner at the Colony, which was the most formal restaurant I had ever seen. The waiters treated Miss Ferber like a grande dame and scarcely noticed the movie star who was her guest. She had seen portions of *Giant* and commended Rock on his performance. "You *are* my Bick Benedict," she declared. Rock couldn't have been happier. He was convinced that *Giant* represented his best work, and he was more impatient than ever for the film to be released. The meticulous George Stevens was still editing, and *Giant* was not scheduled to be premiered until the fall of 1956.

From New York we flew to Paris for the experience of a lifetime.

Universal spared no expense to please its favorite boy and his bride. Our suite at the Plaza Athénée resembled the living quarters of a palace. I had never lived in such opulence—brocaded chairs, magnificent antique chests, inlaid-wood tables, thick oriental carpet, canopied bed with silk sheets, bathroom of pink marble, paintings that looked like old masters on the walls. The hotel employees treated us like royalty. I had to smile when I thought of how within the space of a week I had come from my old room in Montevideo to this palatial suite in the heart of Paris.

"Wow, this is really living!" I exclaimed, and Rock laughed at my exuberance.

A Rolls-Royce limousine was always prepared to take us wherever we wanted to go in Paris. On our first day, we visited all the tourist sights—Arc de Triomphe, Eiffel Tower, Napoleon's tomb, Notre Dame, the Louvre, Sacre Coeur, the Opéra. That night we dined at the Tour d'Argent, where the owner, Claude Terrail, supervised a special meal. Afterward we strolled along the Seine in the moonlight, hand in hand. I don't think Rock and I were ever more in love than on that evening. All Paris had been laid at our feet, and we were enjoying it and each other. I sensed a unique calmness in Rock's soul. The anxieties of his career were thousands of miles away, and he could be himself, not Rock Hudson Movie Star.

On to Rome, where Universal staged a press conference. Rock and I had hardly settled at the Grand Hotel when a company representative said it was time to meet the Italian press. The conference was held in a ballroom that was almost filled with reporters and photographers. Rock charmed them all. Both the questions and his replies had to be translated, and many of his answers brought appreciative laughter. He told them how much he loved Italy, which was true, and how he hoped to make a movie there some day. He introduced me, and the paparazzi took hundreds of photographs.

Rock's official duties over, we could resume our vacation. First, the sights of Rome, with Rock capturing all the views with his movie camera. We also toured the shops, and I must have bought twenty pairs of white gloves. One morning a limousine appeared in front of the hotel, and we loaded our luggage and set out to discover all of Italy.

I don't think we missed a single cathedral or Michelangelo sculpture. The driver, who spoke limited English, insisted on stopping at every place of interest. Rock was fascinated at first, but after about fifty churches, he stayed in the car and let me do the sight-seeing. I was really excited about seeing Venice, and so was Rock. But then he had one of his peeves. I was late in arriving for our gondola ride, and he pouted the whole time. The gondolier took movies of us, and they show how grumpy Rock was.

Florence was another fabulous experience, especially seeing Michelangelo's *David,* the Baptistry doors, and the wonders of the Uffizi gallery. It was a great education in Italian culture, even if my arches did suffer from all those marble floors.

It seemed to be a happy time for Rock. He enjoyed seeing Italy through my curious and eager eyes. He loved the food—couldn't get enough pasta. And he had a degree of freedom, especially outside Rome. Naturally he was a target for stares, as any towering American would be, and often I could tell that he was recognized as Rock Hudson. But although the Italians were friendly, they were never intrusive. They respected our privacy.

We returned to Rome for a few days of rest before departing for Kenya and *Something of Value.*

Rock and I dined one night at Ostaria dell'Orso near the Piazza Navona. It was one of Rome's most famous restaurants, occupying an inn where, they claimed, Dante stayed in the fourteenth century. We had a great dinner and consumed a bottle of Chianti, so we were both feeling no pain.

"Let's go back to the Via Veneto and watch the action," Rock suggested.

"Sounds great!" I agreed.

We found a front table at one of the sidewalk cafés and ordered brandy. The passing parade offered unending entertainment. American tourists in their baggy shorts and flowered shirts. Frizzy-haired whores eyeing the tables for customers. Italian men, their well-tailored coats hung on their shoulders, strolling arm in arm. Many of the passersby recognized Rock, but except for a few stares, he wasn't bothered. He ordered another brandy, and I said, "Why not?" We held hands as we watched the ever-changing scene.

"Oh, hi, Rock."

I looked up and saw a young man with a deeply tanned face and bleached hair. Rock recognized him immediately, shook his hand, and invited him to join us. I could tell he was Italian by his silk suit with scarf at the neck, and he spoke in heavily accented English. Rock introduced me.

"I met him when I was touring Italy after *Captain Lightfoot*," Rock explained.

The Italian kissed my hand with a brief, automatic gesture, then turned his admiring gaze to Rock. They talked on and on while I just sat there, sipping my brandy.

"Tomorrow I'm having lunch with Anna Magnani," the young man said. "I know she'd love to have you and—"

"Phyllis," Rock volunteered.

"—you and Phyllis join us."

"Sounds like fun," Rock said.

By the time the intruder departed, I was annoyed, and a little high. I could tell by the silly grin on his face that Rock was high too. He kept chattering away as we walked through the lobby of the Grand Hotel. I said nothing.

In the elevator he remarked, "That lunch tomorrow sounds like fun."

"I'm not going," I announced.

He looked at me in disbelief. "What do you mean you're not going?" he demanded.

"Just what I said: I'm not going."

The elevator man stared at us, recognizing by the tone of our voices that we were having a spat. As we stepped off at our floor, Rock took me by the arm and turned me toward him. "I want you to tell me why you won't go to the luncheon," he insisted.

"Because I don't want to go!"

"I won't let you go until you tell me the reason."

"Because I don't want to have lunch with him."

"Why don't you want to have lunch with him?"

I hesitated, then blurted, "Because he's a silly little fruitcake."

Whap! Rock's open hand smashed against my face. I was stunned. My necklace broke, scattering pearls all over the hallway. I screamed. I screamed like a two-year-old, loud and shrill. I kept on screaming.

Bellboys came running down the corridor. They saw the situation immediately, a domestic quarrel. One of them led me to the room. Two others took Rock by the arms.

"You're coming with us, Mr. Hudson," a bellboy said. "You can't come back until you've sobered up." They took him away.

I threw myself on the bed, weeping steadily, partly because of the hurt to my cheek by Rock's blow, partly because of the blow to my spirit. How could he do such a thing to his wife? I felt outrage as well as uncomprehending sorrow. It was a long time before I could sleep. A guard sat outside my door all night.

When I woke in the morning, I still couldn't comprehend the events of the night before. Then I remembered another incident. It was at home, and Rock and I had been arguing about something. It couldn't have been terribly important, because I can't remember what the argument concerned. I said something that made him furious. He followed me into the bedroom, put his hands around my neck and started to choke me. He stopped immediately and began to sob. As I held him in my arms, he cried, "I could kill somebody sometime. I have an uncontrollable temper." I comforted him, and the incident was over and forgotten—almost.

This time I didn't know what to think. Yes, he did have an uncontrollable temper; he had proved that to me twice. Yes, it was conceivable that he could kill someone, perhaps even me. Still, he was the man that I had married, the man that I loved. Many wives had to live with violent tempers.

What perplexed me was why he erupted over such a trivial remark. I was still trying to sort it out when I heard a knock, very soft.

Shame was etched on Rock's face. "God, I'm sorry, Bunting," he muttered.

"I'm not going to Africa," I declared. "You go to Africa. Make your damn movie. Just leave me alone. I'm going back to California."

Tears started to flow down his cheeks.

"Don't leave me, Bunting! I couldn't stand it if you left me! I'm sorry, God, how sorry I am. It'll never happen again, I swear it won't."

Was he acting? Was he afraid that the press would uncover the story and the headlines would ruin his career (ROCK HUDSON BEATS WIFE IN ROME HOTEL)? Or did he truly love me and need me to stay with him? If he was acting, he gave an Academy Award performance. I bought it.

14

Africa

I FELT ROTTEN that morning in Rome. Partly it was a wine hangover. But mostly I was hurt and confused, my emotions in a turmoil. Rock had cried and cried, promising that it would never happen again, pleading with me to go to Africa with him. "If you go back to Los Angeles without me, the press will have a banquet out of it," he said. "They'll eat me alive." Was he really contrite, or was he worried about the damage to his career if his wife should arrive in Los Angeles, battered and alone? I was too upset to consider such a question.

My head was aching from the wine, and I still felt the bruise to my cheek. I had cried half the night. I couldn't believe that he had hit me. And over such a trivial matter. So what if I didn't want to have lunch with one of his friends? Why was that so important to him that he would lose his temper and strike me? I still loved him—deeply. But something was off-kilter in our marriage. Why did I not want to be with some of the friends he obviously enjoyed? Why couldn't I simply accept his friends, as most wives do? Something wouldn't allow me to, and although I didn't analyze it, I realized that so many of his friends were a type that didn't appeal to me.

I couldn't find any answers, and my head throbbed from trying. "Yes, I'll go with you," I said. "But I don't feel like it."

Rock agreed that we would visit a friend of mine that day. She was Marchesa Lilli Gereni, whom I had met in New York through my friend Steve Evans. She was now separated from a marchese and living in her villa an hour's drive from Rome. Rock and I got cleaned up, then went downstairs for our limousine. Walking through the lobby was one of the most uncomfortable moments of my life. I was certain that everyone who worked in the hotel had learned of the events of the previous night. I knew they would be whispering, "Signor Hudson was very drunk last night, and he beat his wife." I realized they would be scrutinizing Rock and me to determine if we had kissed and made up, as an Italian husband and wife would. I walked hurriedly, looking neither to the left nor the right, feeling thankful when I reached the open door of the limousine.

Rock tried to make conversation on the drive to the coast, but I wasn't responding, and he finally gave up. Lilli helped bring us out of our funk. She was a marvelous person who seemed to know everyone of importance in Europe and New York and possessed a unique faculty for putting her guests at ease. She gave us a tour of the villa, which had once been owned by Nero, and displayed the collection of gold coins that had been unearthed on her property.

When we were alone, she asked me, "Phyllis, darling, why are you so sad?"

I shrugged. "I'm just tired. Rock and I have been on the go for two weeks."

"No, you're not just tired, you are melancholy. Lilli can tell. Let's take a walk and you can tell me about it."

We strolled along a row of fountains that overlooked the Mediterranean, and I poured out the whole story. Lilli was comforting, but she took a continental attitude. European husbands sometimes struck their wives in a fit of passion, she said, but that didn't mean they were any less in love.

"Do you still love him?" she asked.

"Yes, I think so," I said hesitantly.

"Then stay with him. But be strong."

At dinner I was still somewhat restrained, and Lilli said, "Phyllis, I think you need some music. Do you like Italian music?"

"Of course," I said. She retired to the kitchen to speak to members of her staff. Within half an hour, a dozen gaily costumed musicians appeared with guitars and mandolins, and they serenaded us for an hour with songs like "Santa Lucia" and "Come Back to Sorrento."

It was a bitter farewell to Rome. Universal had arranged a dream tour, and it was just that for most of the two weeks. And then—

I had also noticed a new and disturbing change in Rock. While I was grateful for the luxury of a guided, all-expenses-paid European tour, dining at five-star restaurants and staying at the finest hotels, Rock was not. "Universal owes me this," he said, "after all the money I've made for them." He showed no gratitude for the special courtesies that were accorded him because he was a movie star. They were simply perquisites of his status. He expected everything to be done for him, swiftly and in the best style. He had lost the boyish wonder that I had found so appealing in him.

RICHARD BROOKS, the director and writer of *Something of Value*, stood at the bottom of the steps as we left the plane in Nairobi. The first thing he said was: "There isn't one thing here that won't kill you."

What a welcome to Africa. I was already apprehensive about the trip, since the Mau Mau were still rampaging through parts of Kenya. My concern wasn't helped by all the inoculations we received before leaving California— everything from tetanus to yellow fever. When we were shown to our rooms at the New Stanley Hotel, I found that the twin beds were surrounded by netting. The bellboy said ominously, "You must be careful of mosquitoes. Malaria."

After lunch Rock and I were taken to a tailor's shop to be fitted for safari jackets and pants, then to a bootery for desert boots. "It's good to wear something around your ankles," Brooks warned. "Lots of scorpions around."

"Oh, like Rock," I said. "He's a Scorpio." Rock and I laughed, but Brooks acted as though he hadn't heard the remark. He was a brusque man who always wore a formless flowered shirt and smoked a pipe. With his crew cut and tough talk, he seemed to enjoy reminding people he was once a marine.

Sidney Poitier had arrived the day before, and he joined Brooks, Rock, and me for dinner at the hotel. With his dancing eyes and million-dollar smile, Sidney was wonderful company. Whenever the conversation dragged, he would liven it up with a bright remark.

The dinner was not enjoyable for me. The food was passable, and the waiters were attentive, but I was offended by Richard Brooks's language. Now I had heard all the curse words during my years as a stewardess and in my jobs at New York and Hollywood agencies. But I had never heard such a torrent of obscenities as Brooks poured forth over dinner. Nor did Rock make any move to suggest that such language was not polite in front of his wife.

I finally excused myself and let the three men continue

discussing the movie. During the rest of my stay in Kenya, I declined to eat at the same table with Brooks.

Rock and I had breakfast together in the morning, then he left with other members of the company to scout locations. I decided to walk around the city.

The area near the hotel was filled with shops offering merchandise for tourists. I saw zebra-skin rugs, large statues of natives and animals carved in dark wood, necklaces and bracelets with lions' teeth and warthog tusks, elephant-foot wastebaskets, huge ivory tusks, hand-printed fabrics. All of the shops were operated by Indians, and the streets seemed to contain as many Indians as blacks. The Indians would chew betel nuts and spit in the street.

Returning to the New Stanley Hotel, I encountered a couple of Englishwomen who invited me to join them for lunch. They were wives of army colonels, and throughout the meal they filled me with tales of Mau Mau horror. Settler families, including women and children, hacked to death with machetes. Women raped and murdered while their husbands watched. By the end of lunch I was ready to book a flight to Los Angeles.

"By all means, never go out on the streets alone," one of the women warned.

"You mean right here in Nairobi?" I asked.

"Absolutely. The Mau Mau are here too, and they can strike when you least expect it."

Oh, dear, I thought. Here I was strolling around the city that morning, alone and unsuspecting. I worried that Rock would be angry because of my foolhardiness. He never liked me to go anywhere that he didn't know about or talk to anyone he was unaware of.

After a few days in Nairobi, we drove to the slopes of Mount Kenya, which rose majestically seventeen thousand feet into the ice-blue African sky. The film company was being quartered at the Mawingo Hotel, owned by Jack Block, who also operated the New Stanley in Nairobi. It was a stately place that had been built in the 1930s as a residence for a wealthy and eccentric Englishwoman. When she tired of Africa and her lover, she gave the place to him and returned to England. Later it was sold to Block, who modernized it and changed it into a hotel for safari hunters. In 1960 it was bought by William Holden and two partners, and it became famous as the Mount Kenya Safari Club.

I could see why Jack Block welcomed the *Something of Value* company to the Mawingo (which meant Cloudland). Tourist business had dwindled to almost nothing because of the Mau Mau uprising. The Nanyuki area was the stronghold of the rebel leader, Jomo Kenyatta, who later became Kenya's leader when the country achieved independence from Great Britain.

Rock and I were ushered to the honeymoon suite, which is described in Ruark's book. It was amazing to find such elegance in the heart of Africa—closets and drawers lined in blue satin, oriental rugs, a big four-poster bed. French doors led to the terrace and a staggering view of Mount Kenya. But we were told: "You must never leave the doors open while you sleep. Mau Mau."

From the terrace I could see a trout stream a quarter mile away. "You must not go there without a guard," I was told.

Aside from the movie people, the only other guests at the hotel were English army officers and their wives and a few Americans who lived in Nairobi and came to work in the film. While Rock was off on location, I became acquainted with the army wives, and two of them invited me to play golf. They assured me that the course was well guarded. Besides, the caddies carried rifles in the golf bags.

The clubhouse loaned me a set of clubs, and I enjoyed having the first real exercise since I left California. On the second tee, I sliced a ball into the long grass that bordered the fairway. I followed the caddie into the grass, and we hunted for the ball until he screamed; "Mamba! Black mamba!" The clubs went flying as he leaped out of the grass and headed for the fairway. I didn't know what he was hollering about, but I decided it was wise to follow him. Later I learned that the black mamba is a snake whose bite can kill in an instant.

Rock returned to the hotel every night, hot, dirty, and tired from the day's location. His hair was red from the dust, and he said he felt as if the African dust had invaded every pore. He spent an hour under the shower trying to get clean.

We went downstairs for dinner, but I didn't eat with the production company. All the talk was about the next day's shooting, and I didn't want to hear any more of Richard Brooks's obscenities. Instead, I joined an Englishman named Paul Wells, a delightful man who was doing some still photography on the movie. He had impeccable manners, and he told fascinating stories about his travels around the world. Sometimes Sidney Poitier joined us, remarking, "The conversation is much more interesting over here." Sidney made no secret of the fact that he didn't enjoy the danger of the location. "In fact," he admitted, "every night before I go to sleep, I pull the dresser in front of the door."

Brooks, on the other hand, took a macho attitude toward the whole situation. He seemed almost to be inviting trouble, perhaps because he thrived on it, perhaps because he thought the publicity would be good for the movie. One Sunday, the only day off for the film workers, he took Rock and others into the mountains to meet the Mau Mau. I was furious when they returned.

"How could you do anything so dangerous?" I demanded of Rock.

"Oh, it wasn't as bad as all that," he replied. "Those Mau Mau seem like nice people."

"Nice people! They're killers!"

Rock remained unconcerned. To him it was just part of the make-believe of making movies.

Each day I lunched with the officers' wives, and each day

they provided me with horror stories. The Mau Mau came out of the mountains at night, killed the cattle, and carried off what they needed. They never lighted fires, and they were impossible to track. The settler families never knew whom they could trust. Usually one of the servants was a Mau Mau or a sympathizer, and he would leave a door unlocked. All the family members would be killed in their beds. At dinner, I was told, the husband of a family always sat at the table with a rifle in his lap.

"My dear," said one of the English ladies, "if you stay here long enough, you'll equip yourself with one of these." She opened her purse and showed me a small pistol.

All their stories made me nervous and edgy. One day I was washing my hands in the bathroom when the male attendant entered the suite. I could see him out of the corner of my eye as he approached. Then I saw two arms above me, and I screamed. The poor man jumped and ran out of the suite. He was only placing fresh towels in the racks.

After that, I decided it was foolish to be so frightened of a people who appeared to be so gentle and eager to be friendly. I learned a few words of Swahili and went out of my way to communicate with them. They seemed genuinely pleased.

While Rock was on location, I played gin rummy with other hotel guests or I sat in my room and read. The hotel had some tame monkeys on the grounds, and sometimes I played with them. I visited the movie set a few times, but I never stayed long. Richard Brooks didn't want any visitors. He appeared to resent having outsiders observe him at work. Although Rock seemed pleased when I arrived, he always gave me the impression that he didn't want me to stay. Perhaps he thought the location was too dirty for me.

One day when Rock wasn't working, we drove to a game preserve. Both of us were dressed in our safari outfits, and I felt a sense of adventure, as if I were Ernest Hemingway's bride, venturing into lion country in an open Jeep. But we encountered no real danger, and Rock shot reels of movies of the baboons, giraffes, zebra, gazelles, etc.

I really think Rock was trying to make up for what happened in Rome. He was much more attentive than he had been, and he repeatedly said, "I don't know why I did it." But whenever I tried to discuss the problems of our relationship, he simply said, "I don't want to talk about it." And I would face a stone wall.

I wasn't feeling well in Africa. Partly, I suppose, I was still in shock over the event in Rome. Also, the jet flights and the constant touring had drained my energy. I had never fully recovered from the auto accident in New York. All the walking around Europe and Africa had made my leg ache.

"I want to go home," I told Rock. He didn't urge me to stay, even though he had another week or so of location filming. He gave me a tender farewell as I boarded a light plane for Nairobi, from which I flew to Stockholm. I took the fastest way home, an over-the-pole SAS flight. I sat next to a Los Angeles businessman who introduced me to akvavit. It was yummy. As the plane approached LAX, I had a warm feeling of contentment. I was coming home.

15

Box-Office King

LOS ANGELES never looked so good to me as it did when I returned on the SAS flight. I was thrilled to be back in my own home, surrounded by the things I loved. I had worried that Demi might forget me, but he greeted me with more than his usual excitement. How sweet it was to sleep in my own bed, but I missed having Rock beside me. I could even have tolerated his heavy arm across my chest.

Rock returned two weeks later. I thought he would come home sooner, but he explained that he had to stop in New York to discuss a movie deal with someone. "For five days?" I asked. He said it was an important movie.

He went to work immediately at MGM, filming the interior scenes of *Something of Value*. He finished shooting in early October 1956, and apparently he would have several months off. That was good news to me. Rock had been working in one picture after another ever since I met him, and I felt that placed too much strain on our marriage. We needed time to be by ourselves, to travel without the obligations of publicity or locations, to solve our differences and create a firm foundation for our marriage. At least that was my hope.

Henry had other plans for Rock.

"You're gonna be the number-one star in Hollywood, I can feel it," Henry told Rock. *"Written on the Wind* is doing great business, and your reviews were terrific. Those were nothing compared to what you'll get for *Giant.* Then you've got *Battle Hymn*—a one-two-three punch! We're gonna go for all the marbles—every magazine story you can do, all the magazine covers, every p.a. the studios want to send you on. This is it, Rock, what we've been dreaming of!"

Rock swallowed it whole. I tried to avoid throwing up. It seemed to me that if Rock was such a big star he should have been earning more money—and keeping it. Even with my limited access to his finances, I could see that his earnings were not commensurate with those of other stars of less box-office power. I knew nothing of his investments, if any.

Whenever I mentioned such matters, Rock always shut me off: "Those are things for Henry and me to decide." As far as I could see, Henry was making all the decisions, and I wasn't sure they were to Rock's advantage.

My hopes of time for Rock and me to be alone together went unrealized. The Universal publicity department scheduled interviews almost every day. Often Rock would telephone late in the afternoon and say, "Honey, I'm doing an interview so I might be a little late getting home. Don't worry, I'll be home in time for dinner." I suspected that the little message was delivered in the presence of the interviewer.

Sometimes I was a trifle surprised when I read the fan

magazine stories. Like the one titled "When Day Is Done—Heaven Is Waiting."

"No one should live alone," Rock Hudson says, out of the blissful depths of his still-new marriage. "Now that I have Phyllis to share life with, I'll never have to experience that bottomless pit of loneliness again. It's a very comfortable feeling."

Phyllis, who's feeling fairly comfortable herself, is a wise wife, and thus far has said nothing for publication, letting Mr. Hudson speak for both of 'em. He's the boss, he's the voice, he wears the pants.

"Phyllis doesn't have any career association," Rock says. (Phyllis used to be an agent.) "She quit right after we got married. I wouldn't let her do anything outside even if she wanted to. When I got married, it was my idea to have a home, and a wife at home."

The lady cooks, never demands to be taken to nightclubs, and is saving beyond belief. Rock bought her an expensive tablecloth, and she admired it: "How lovely!" Then: "I'll take it back and get five others for it."

The Hudsons plan lots of babies and lots of travel, with the travel to come first, when the babies aren't around to impede same. Rock, having had no brothers or sisters himself, feels keenly the plight of the only child, and wants a houseful of screaming, laughing offspring . . .

"When I count my blessings," Rock says today, "and there are many, my marriage tops the list. This realization sweeps over me when day is done, and I head for home. I know Phyllis is there, and I can only say, she was worth waiting for . . ."

Except that many times he didn't head for home. In late afternoon came the telephone call: "I'm talking business with Henry. Don't know how long I'll be. You go ahead and eat." When he came home hours later, he explained that he had already had dinner.

Here are excerpts from another fan magazine story titled "Trapped, Feeling No Pain."

"Marriage," Rock told me sincerely, "has turned out to be all I hoped for, and more. I'm just a whole lot happier. It's really great."

Rock waxed almost poetic on the subject.

"I have a permanent feeling," he smiled as he pulled out a pack of cigarettes and offered me one. "I feel the security— you know, the stuff you hate to talk about. Serene? No, I wouldn't use that word. Serene sounds like you're living in a violin case, like you're swans on a duck pond. I don't know how I'd put it." He thought a second, then found an analogy. "Like fire in a fireplace, I'd say . . ."

Before their marriage, Phyllis's freshness and vivacity had frequently been remarked upon by enchanted observers of the Hollywood scene. I made so bold as to ask if the rigors of marriage had even imperceptibly dampened her appealing ardor that used to delight everyone.

"She's more vibrant and vivacious than ever," Rock proclaimed happily.

She is in every sense of the word mistress of their home. She not only presides over the pots and pans, but over their social life and over the everyday chores that make married life pleasant and livable. She gathers up best-sellers for Rock at bookstores, classical recordings at music stores, and has warm meals ready for him when he gets home after a tough day at the studio. Phyllis even knows exactly how to handle her handsome spouse in those off-moments when he's not his charming best.

"I'm really moody," Rock confessed, "and I'm difficult to get along with when I'm moody. I don't say anything. After she finds out I'm moody, she just lets me alone, and it works out fine. There are little things between a husband and wife nobody else would understand or cope with . . ."

At least the article got one thing right. His moods. They became deeper and more impenetrable after the return from Africa. Our lovemaking became more routine and perfunctory. Because of my farm upbringing, I guess, I like to rise early and go to bed early. Rock was nocturnal. When we first were married, both of us compromised so we could go to bed at the same time. After Africa, I went to sleep alone more and more of the time. Rock had disappeared into the storage room to edit his movies. He remained there for hours, huddled over his editing machine.

Yet there were times when the honeymoon passion returned, and we had good times in bed. Rock's moodiness would disappear. "I think marriage agrees with me, I feel so good," he said.

At such times he seemed to appreciate the stability that a wife and home provided. He liked to entertain our friends and brag about my cooking. There were periods when he liked my cooking too much. Rock ate like a growing boy; he loved chili, hot dogs, hamburgers, downed with quarts of milk. But he wasn't growing upward anymore. He tried to keep his weight at 185 pounds, but at one point he ballooned to 235. I changed my cooking style, eliminating the starchy, fattening foods and providing tasty, nutritional things. In time his weight returned to normal.

Rock enjoyed having me at his side during the many premieres, banquets, parties, and industry events we attended in late 1956. For all his movie-star charm, he retained a certain shyness, and he seemed to gain a degree of confidence by having me on his arm as we posed for the phalanx of photographers.

The events came swiftly. On September 7 we'd attended the premiere of *Written on the Wind,* for which Rock drew raves for his dramatic performance. On September 26, Rock and Elizabeth Taylor planted their hand- and footprints in the cement at Grauman's Chinese Theater. In early October, Rock and I flew to New York for the world premiere of *Giant* at the Roxy Theater. The Warner Brothers publicity department created a whirlwind of excitement for the premiere, and Rock was racing from one interview and television appearance to another, as were other members of the *Giant* cast. Every hour was booked, and we attended lunches at "21," receptions, cocktail parties, etc.

On the evening of October 10, Rock and I left the Waldorf-Astoria in a limousine, headed for the Roxy. It took an hour to get there through the crowded streets, and for the last three blocks we inched along, the limousine windows filled with wild-eyed, shouting faces. When we finally stepped out in front of the theater, the noise was deafening.

"Phyllis, how are you?" said George Stevens, Sr., as Rock was being interviewed on television. I thought, what a kind and thoughtful man, to seek me out during all the hoopla over his epic movie.

Rock finished running the gauntlet, and we were ushered to our seats in the huge theater. I sat enthralled through the entire three hours and twenty-one minutes of *Giant*, never wanting it to end. When it was over, I threw my arms around Rock and kissed him. I had never been so proud of him.

Henry Willson was even more ecstatic. At the post-premiere party, he was overcome with joy; you'd think *he* had played Bick Benedict, not Rock. The next day I thought it would be fun to escape the noise and clamor and take a drive to New England to see the autumn foliage. Henry hired a limo, and the three of us rode to Connecticut and had dinner at a lovely old inn. Henry was still on a high from the premiere, telling Rock that *Giant* was going to make him the biggest star in Hollywood, that he was certain to win an Academy Award, etc. On the trip back to New York, Henry was quite drunk, but he insisted on stopping every few miles at a tavern. Both Rock and I were also exhilarated, and I allowed Henry to introduce me to B&Bs. I got sick on the drive back to New York.

The Hollywood premiere of *Giant* was held at Grauman's Chinese Theater a week later, and it was an equal triumph. Again the limo picked us up, again the fans clamored on the last blocks to the theater. I could tell by Rock's flushed cheeks how excited he was. We sat next to Elizabeth Taylor and Michael Wilding in the theater, and

Rock and I held hands throughout the movie, squeezing to indicate our appreciation of certain scenes. Both of us felt that he had reached a new peak in his career.

The party after the premiere was held in the Crystal Room of the Beverly Hills Hotel, and both Rock and Elizabeth were greeted by lightning flashes from the fan magazine photographers. During all the excitement I had one moment of sorrow. I thought of James Dean and how he tried to teach me to spin a lariat in Texas. How sad it was that he couldn't be there to share the glory.

WITH ALL THE ACTIVITY going on in Rock's career, there wasn't much time left for our personal life. But we did manage to give a few dinners. Sidney Poitier came to dinner a couple of times. He always arrived with a broad smile and the question: "How was your day, Phyllis?" Unlike some actors I had known, he listened intently to what I had to say. In the late Indian summer, we barbecued steaks outside. One night I was in the kitchen when I heard Sidney tell Rock, "It's very important, Rock, to make yourself interested in what your wife does. We get too caught up in our careers. They must feel important too." During the evenings he spent at our house, I confirmed what I had felt about Sidney in Africa: that he was a warm, compassionate human being with a sincere interest in the feelings of those he met. He was sensitive and caring, and worried about how other people felt.

As the date of our wedding anniversary approached, I wondered how Rock and I would celebrate. I would have enjoyed a quiet dinner at L'Escoffier. I should have known that the anniversary would turn into a Henry Willson Production.

"I'm going to give you two the biggest party this town has seen in years," Henry promised. And that's about what he did.

The party cost him ten thousand dollars, a figure he liberally disclosed to the columnists who were invited. First of all, he hired the United Tent Company to erect a circus-size tent at the back of his Stone Canyon house, covering over the swimming pool for a bandstand and dance floor. The tent had celluloid sides so the guests could gaze into Henry's garden, which was bathed in blue light.

The lawn was dotted with tables covered with deep-pink tablecloths and topped with bowls of American Beauty roses. Three bars had been set up at ends of the tent, and Chasen's had been hired to cater the dinner. The guests were dressed in black tie and evening dresses.

And what a guest list. Henry insisted that Rock and I stand at the entrance and receive the guests, just like at a wedding reception. I saw more stars than at a movie pre-miere. Barbara Stanwyck came through alone, and she told Rock: "I saw *Giant,* and you were the only actor who aged convincingly." Rock blushed at such a tribute.

Jennifer Jones was there with David O. Selznick; they seldom went to parties, but he wanted Rock to star with his wife in *A Farewell to Arms.* Ginger Rogers came with her husband, Jacques Bergerac, a French charmer who gave me more than the customary kiss. Greg Bautzer escorted his bride, the exquisite Dana Wynter. George Nader's date for the evening was Martha Hyer. Diana Dors and Marie Wilson competed for the lowest-cut evening gown. Gary Cooper's wife Rocky appeared with two escorts, the grand-son of the king of Italy and the race car driver Stirling Moss. Among the other stars I remember were Rhonda Fleming, Dorothy Malone, Corinne Calvet, and Virginia Grey.

Henry was careful to invite the power structure of Holly-wood, men who could hire his clients. They included Dore Schary of MGM, Buddy Adler of 20th Century-Fox, as well as William Goetz, Mervyn LeRoy, Al Zugsmith, and Aaron Rosenberg.

I certainly didn't expect to be noticed in this stellar crowd, but one of the columnists wrote afterward:

It touched me that this was the shy Rock I knew so many years ago, the loyal Rock who stuck with the same agent even after he hit the big time, the so-in-love Rock who could hardly take his eyes off Phyllis.

I have never seen her look so radiantly beautiful. She was in a mauve-colored dinner dress, and somehow it set off her coloring as never before. Phyllis has a radiant peaches-and-cream skin; the kind that blooms with health and is innocent of makeup. She is the only woman since Bergman to look glamorous with only a touch of makeup . . .

As Rock grows in stature as a man and as an actor, as his wife remains womanly, unaffected, and "un-Hollywood," it does something to your heart. You're suddenly reminded that miracles do happen. That people are nice. That friends remain friends.

At midnight waiters carried in a huge cake—"almost as tall as Rock," said one of the reporters. Rock and I cut the first slice, then the orchestra struck up "The Anniversary Waltz." (My husband was a wonderful dancer, but if we danced too long, sometimes my neck got stiff from looking up!) Rock glided me over the dance floor amid the applause of the guests, and I found myself almost believing that miracles do happen. I felt transported back to the night when we first danced at L'Escoffier.

Rock had remained at my side all evening, holding my hand, clutching me, gazing fondly in my eyes. After "The Anniversary Waltz," he danced with his mother, who was almost speechless over the glamour of the occasion. I was invited to dance by several guests, including a tall, dark-haired young man who bore a striking resemblance to Rock.

"I'm John Gavin, one of Henry's clients," he smiled.

"Oh, *you're* the one," I said.

"The one what?"

"Henry told me he got you a contract at Universal—so you can be in the bull pen in case Rock makes trouble."

John laughed. "I wouldn't mind doing Rock's castoffs.

But I'll never be a threat to him." Nor could Henry use him as such. John left the Willson Agency after a year.

It was a magnificent evening, for which Henry provided an anticlimax. He didn't want to waste the tent and the flowers, so the following night he gave another party, this time for his "B list" of guests. They included his lesser clients, plus a lot of young men. Henry insisted that Rock and I make an appearance, but I was tired, and we left early.

Rock and I had our own private celebration of our wedding anniversary. Since the first is the paper anniversary, I had to use my imagination for a gift Rock would enjoy. When he opened his package, he found a pair of light blue boxer shorts—his favorite color—stuffed with dollar bills. He thought that was hilarious.

Rock's present to me was the most thoughtful gift I could imagine. Unbeknown to me, Rock had been taking photographs of my poodle Demi. He selected the ones that captured Demi's unique personality. He went to the advertising agency where Pat Devlin worked and spent hours with layout artists devising an album. All of the captions were written by Rock and printed in gold. "Dear Mommie" was inscribed on the cover, and Demi's pawprint was on the lower right corner. Needless to say, I was thrilled with the album, and I cherish it still.

FOR ROCK'S thirty-first birthday, Henry wanted to take us to dinner at Romanoff's. "I'm tired, can't we stay home, honey?" Rock asked me. "Your cooking is better than Romanoff's. You can make me a chocolate soufflé." I told him, "We can't disappoint Henry. He has already invited some other people and has ordered a special cake."

The dinner reflected Henry's excellent taste. He had ordered a special duck dish with Bing cherries, and the wine was Puligny-Montrachet. Henry kept the conversation lively, and Rock enjoyed himself despite being tired.

When we got home, I gave Rock his birthday presents: cashmere sweaters, shirts, ties, pajamas.

For my birthday, Rock gave me clothes, as well as a pearl necklace and bracelet. He loved seeing my delight when I opened his gifts. Every time he went shopping, he brought me home something.

The holidays were full of activities. Kay and Joe Olsen came to Christmas dinner at our house. David and Jennifer Selznick invited us to their New Year's Eve party. On New Year's Day, Rock and I held an open house. Dozens of people streamed in and out of the house all day. Rock volunteered to make the eggnog, which he served in a beautiful silver punch bowl with twelve silver cups, a wedding present from Henry.

Both of us made all kinds of New Year's resolutions, none of which we could remember the next day. With the birthdays and anniversary and holidays, I had a good feeling about our marriage, and I think Rock felt the same way. These were times when he enjoyed being a husband and having a home.

The new year brought an unforeseen accolade to Rock. The theater owners of America voted him the number-one money-making star, placing him ahead of John Wayne, Pat Boone, Elvis Presley, Frank Sinatra, and Gary Cooper.

"I can't believe it!" Rock exclaimed.

"I can," Henry Willson said with a self-satisfied smile. "It's what I've been planning all along."

16

A Farewell to Arms

IN JANUARY, my mother and father came to California for the first time. I chose a time when Rock was going to be gone on a personal appearance tour because I knew it would be crowded in our small, one-bathroom house. He came back early, but it worked out satisfactorily, at first.

I had a great time showing Mom and Dad all the sights. I took them to the Farmers Market, to the beach, to the department stores, to lovely restaurants for lunch. Rock invited them to lunch at the studio, and he took them on some of the movie sets.

"I'm going to give a party for your parents and Rock's parents," Henry announced. He planned the dinner with his usual thoroughness, inviting his own father as well as some of the older stars and character actors. It was a pleasant evening, and Henry exercised his charm on the older folks to make them feel at ease. He could be very funny, and Mom was amused by him. Dad wasn't. "There's something the matter with that man," he told me.

In the days following the party, Rock fell into one of his moody spells, making it uncomfortable for my parents. They made no complaint, but they decided to cut short their Los Angeles vacation. I think they were happy to return to the Minnesota winter.

Rock was not easy to live with in early 1957. While he wasn't bigheaded about being king of the box office, Henry kept reminding him of his status and promulgating plans to keep him there. Henry was all atwitter, reporting each offer from a major studio to borrow Rock at his going price of $400,000 a picture, a huge amount for 1957. Henry had accepted the deal from David O. Selznick for Rock to appear opposite Jennifer Jones in *A Farewell to Arms,* a remake of the Ernest Hemingway novel to be directed by John Huston. Henry had formed a production company, in which he and Rock were partners with Henry Ginsberg, the former production chief at Paramount and coproducer with George Stevens of *Giant.* Rock had presented me a 5 percent interest in the company as a Christmas present.

The added responsibilities seemed to make Rock edgier, more restless. On weekends he would say, "I'm going over to Mark and George's to play basketball." He would be gone all day. Sometimes Henry invited us to his house for a swimming party. There would always be a group of boys there, talking about trivial matters and playing childish games in the pool. I gave up going.

Our lovemaking had improved since Dr. Brandsma prescribed the salve. But there were fewer times when Rock would grin and say, "Wanna play?"

Occasionally I received telephone calls during the day, young male voices asking, "Is Rock there?" When I said he wasn't, the answer would be, "Tell him Jim called." Or, "Just say Roger called." When I asked Rock about the messages, he said, "Oh, they must be fans. We'd better get the phone number changed again." It still seemed odd to me that he would be receiving so many similar calls. But they stopped after our number was changed.

In February, Rock was scheduled to make a tour for openings of *Battle Hymn* in the East. Jack Diamond, head of publicity at Universal, suggested that I accompany Rock. "The fans and reporters are interested in you, too, Phyllis," he said. "It would be good for you to go along."

Rock agreed, but when we were alone, he repeated what he had often said, "Remember, I don't want you talking to the press. *I'll* do all the talking." Agreed. I was still shy about speaking to reporters, and even if I wasn't, the brain-washing by Rock and Henry had conditioned me.

As usual, I helped Rock pack for the trip, folding his shirts so they wouldn't wrinkle. With all the appearances he would be making, he needed many changes of clothes. I enjoyed getting out the handsome suits he had received from movie roles; I knew how great he would look in them. I had to pack a variety of my outfits, too. Happily, Universal would pay for the airline overweight.

First stop, Chicago, where the press made much of the fact that Rock was a hometown boy—Winnetka, anyway. Then to Marietta, Ohio, Dean Hess's hometown, for the world premiere of *Battle Hymn*. Marietta College presented Rock with an honorary degree in the humanities, and at the time I thought that was quite an honor. Only years later, when I myself was struggling to earn a degree, did I realize what an empty gesture that was.

On to New York for the *Battle Hymn* opening there.

When we were in New York on our honeymoon, Rock and I had enjoyed a degree of privacy. That had changed. In a little over a year, Rock had risen to superstar, and the crowds reacted accordingly. We were followed everywhere by screaming teenagers. They tried to tear Rock's clothes. They grabbed at my hair. "Oh, Rock, we love you!" they yelled. Rock was supposed to make an appearance in the lobby of the Capitol Theater. The crowd was so thick and unruly that the police wouldn't allow him there. He had to sneak in the side entrance and appear on the stage instead.

I hated the crowds. I felt endangered as they swarmed around us. I worried that we both would be crushed and trampled to death. What a relief it was to finally reach the quiet and privacy of the hotel suite.

Rock became snarly toward the fans. He stared right past them, ignoring their entreaties for autographs.

"Why can't you sign a few of them and then move on?" I suggested. "They're your fans, Rock. Be nice to them. You'll need them later on."

"They're morons," he snapped, and that was the end of it.

Boston was almost as clamorous. Universal had arranged for Rock to appear before two thousand teenage girls at a Heart Fund benefit at John Hancock Hall. The girls started lining up before dawn, and by the time Rock and I walked onstage, pandemonium ensued. Rock introduced me and gave me a big kiss, causing a wave of ooohs and aaahs.

Rock was supposed to answer questions from the audience, but it was hard for him to be heard amid the noise. He was asked his favorite movie actress. "Ingrid Bergman," he replied. His favorite movie? *"Giant."* For two hours Rock replied to questions, his answers punctuated with shrieks and howls.

When it was finally over, Boston police conferred on how to get Rock away from the mob. They decided to use me as a decoy, sending me to the limousine first, surrounded by officers. The girls were not easily fooled, and when Rock emerged, they sent up a shrill cry and raced in his direction. A flying wedge of policemen struggled to get Rock to the limo.

That night we were relaxing at a nightclub when a group of reporters approached our table. "You've been nominated for an Academy Award," one of them announced.

Rock leaped up with a whoop, then gave me a hug and

kiss. "I'm overwhelmed," he told the reporters. "I still can't believe it. This has been the biggest week of my life!"

I was glowing with pride for him. I knew how hard Rock had worked to improve himself as an actor and how he felt inferior to actors with years of stage training. Rock had done it all in films, working his way up from bit parts and potboilers. Now he had achieved the highest honor from his fellow actors: an Academy Award nomination. "I'm so thrilled for you!" I exclaimed. James Dean was also nominated for Best Actor of 1956. Elizabeth Taylor was not nominated.

The next stop on the tour was Washington, where the Korean ambassador to the United States hosted a dinner at the embassy; Colonel Hess had been a hero of the Korean War. On to Pittsburgh, where the pocket of my coat was ripped off in a mob scene. Throughout the tour I had maintained my equilibrium, smiling as I held the bouquet of flowers that greeted me at every stop. I adhered to Rock's dictum not to talk to reporters. Sometimes it wasn't easy, because the reporters seemed as eager to talk to me as to Rock. One reporter in Washington pursued me relentlessly, but I managed to escape without providing him with any copy.

Toward the end of the tour, I wasn't feeling well. I suspected that I was simply run-down because of the hectic pace Rock and I had been keeping up. I ordered sundaes in our suite, thinking they would increase my energy. They also were soothing to my sore stomach.

By the time we returned to New York, I felt rotten. In our suite in the Waldorf Towers I kept running to the bathroom to throw up. Rock wasn't around. Even though he had fulfilled his obligations to Universal, he said he had a lot of appointments with magazine editors and other people. When he returned to the hotel, he saw how pale I looked.

"I'm sick," I said. "I think I need to see a doctor."

Rock telephoned for the house physician, who diagnosed my problem as food poisoning. "I don't wonder," he said, "considering all the places you've been and the food you've eaten."

"Yes," I said, "but Rock ate the same things I did, and he's okay."

"Food poisoning affects different people in different ways," the doctor said. "You appear to be exhausted, while your husband seems able to survive on all the activity."

I wasn't so sure of his reasoning, but I welcomed his prescription of rest and Coke syrup to calm my stomach. It was the first time during our marriage that I had been sick, and I was bitterly disappointed by Rock's indifference. He continued with his appointments, leaving me alone for hours at a time.

I was miserable on the flight home. The only thing that helped me was drinking Cokes, lots of Cokes. Tony Bennett, the singer, sat across the aisle, and he was very concerned about my health. "She'll be all right as soon as she gets home," Rock assured.

ROCK WAS RIGHT. I did feel better after I returned to our cozy house and my darling Demi. The show biz life was exciting and glamorous, but I was more comfortable waking up in the morning knowing where I was.

Coming home hadn't changed Rock's attitude. He was still cool and hard to reach. I thought we could have some fun in the three weeks before he was scheduled to leave for Italy to begin *A Farewell to Arms*. But he insisted that he had to work full days at the studio, having tests and wardrobe fittings and giving interviews.

"Can't you at least call me sometime during the day?" I asked rather plaintively. "You know, it gets lonely here when you're away all the time."

During this time I had friends tell me, "Oh, I saw Rock in Santa Monica today." Or, "I saw Rock in Westwood." I told them, "You must have seen someone who looked like him. Rock's at the studio all day."

One day Rock came home with several new pairs of blue jeans. I was appalled. "Where did you buy those—J. C. Penney's?" I asked. He was bad enough in those cotton pants he loved to wear. Jeans I couldn't tolerate.

"Are you kidding?" he said defensively. "These are top-of-the-line Levi's."

"They're bottom of the barrel, as far as I'm concerned. I hate them. Why can't you wear gray flannel, like Fred Astaire? You look great in *good* clothes."

He wouldn't listen. He filled the kitchen sink and threw a pair of the jeans into the water. "What are you doing?" I asked.

"A wrangler at the studio told me how to get 'em to fit," Rock said. "You're supposed to soak 'em and wear 'em wet. Then they fit the contours of your body."

For days he wore those tight-fitting jeans until I couldn't stand it. When he was gone, I gathered them all and went out to the backyard incinerator, which we had in Los Angeles until the smog laws outlawed them. I crumpled some newspapers, threw in the jeans, and lit a match. They made a nice fire.

Rock was furious. "Have you lost your marbles?" he ranted. "How *dare* you destroy my property! That's the shittiest thing I ever heard of!"

I guess it was a mistake. Rock didn't talk to me for three days. I didn't know why I did it. Frustration, perhaps. Maybe I thought an extreme act would get his attention; if so, it didn't work. I realized later that my problem wasn't merely annoyance with Rock. I was really sick.

Rock and I met Pat and Rux for dinner at Dino's Lodge on the Sunset Strip. Around other people Rock could be charming and funny, and I enjoyed seeing that side of him for a change. But midway through dinner, I began to feel clammy and faint. "Rock, I think I'm going to be sick," I said. I rushed to the ladies' room just in time. I apologized to Pat and Rux for spoiling the party. Rock took me home.

I marshaled all my energies in the week remaining before Rock had to leave for Italy. It wasn't easy to run all his errands and get his shirts washed and ironed and his shoes shined and pack his bags when the thing I wanted to do most was lie down in bed. I knew if I didn't do those things, they wouldn't get done. Rock would never see to it.

On the morning of March 8 the studio limousine arrived outside our door. I supervised the loading of Rock's bags into the trunk.

"Don't you want to ride to the airport with me?" Rock asked.

"No, I'm afraid I might throw up in the limo. That wouldn't be a very nice send-off."

We walked out to the car, and Rock turned and hugged me. "I'm gonna miss you, Bunting," he said.

"Me, too." I tried unsuccessfully to stop the tears from flowing.

"Now remember, if you need anything, just call Florence Kelly, and she'll take care of it," he said, referring to Henry Willson's accountant. "She's a little on the fuddy-duddy side, but don't pay any attention to her."

We kissed, and Rock entered the limo. I stood at the top of the driveway and waved to him as the limo backed down the hill. He telephoned from the airport to say that he was sorry I couldn't go with him and that I should join him as soon as I felt better. He sounded so endearing that I began to cry again. I realized how deeply I loved him and how saddened I was by his departure. How could I have known that it was the beginning of the end?

17

"Please, Honey, Can't You Come Home?"

I REMAINED IN BED for two days after Rock left for Italy. I felt miserable, but I attributed that to loneliness for Rock. On Wednesday I realized I was physically ill, and I gathered up my strength to go see Dr. Brandsma. He had been concerned about my health for months. Every time he saw me, he remarked, "You look tired, Phyllis."

When I appeared in his office on that Wednesday, he was alarmed. "I don't like your color, Phyllis," he said. "I want to take some tests."

Dr. Brandsma called me the following day. "I want you to enter the hospital," he said.

My heart began to pound. Did he have some terrible news for me?

"When do you want me to go?" I asked.

"Tomorrow morning. St. John's."

"What's wrong with me, Dr. Brandsma?"

"I don't know yet, Phyllis. But when we find out, we'll get you well again."

The next morning was Friday, and Steve Evans, the friend who had convinced me to come to California, drove me to the hospital.

After a bewildering number of tests, my trouble was diagnosed: hepatitis—*infectious* hepatitis. Dr. Brandsma ordered nurses around the clock and intravenous feeding because I couldn't keep anything in my stomach. I was given vitamin shots daily and a tranquilizer every four hours to combat my severe depression. I was scarcely aware of what was happening, I was so sick. The one thing that concerned me was Demi.

"My dog," I moaned. "Someone has to take care of my dog."

"Don't you worry, Mrs. Hudson," the nun said. "Your friends are seeing to that."

Steve Evans and Pat Devlin had rallied to my support. They alternated spending nights at my house so Demi would be cared for. They were the only two visitors Dr. Brandsma allowed. Each would drive to St. John's and stay with me a few minutes, as long as they were permitted. They were required to wear hospital gowns and masks because of the infection.

I wasn't allowed a telephone in my room, so Dr. Brandsma volunteered to notify Rock. He sent a cable to the film location on the day I entered the hospital.

After two weeks, my physical strength was returning, but I was depressed. What troubled me most was that I had received no word from Rock. "Dr. Brandsma, why don't I hear from him?" I asked.

"I don't know," he replied. "I'll call him when I get back to my office."

Later Dr. Brandsma, who can be a blunt Dutchman, related the conversation:

BRANDSMA: Rock, what the hell is the matter with you? I cabled you two weeks ago that your wife is seriously ill in the hospital, and she hasn't heard a word from you!

ROCK: Oh, God, I *am* sorry. I've been so busy on this damn picture.

BRANDSMA: That's a damn feeble excuse. Rock, you should be ashamed of yourself.

ROCK: I am. I am. I'll do something about it right away.

That day I received a dozen red roses from Rock. He called that evening, and the nurse installed a phone in my room so I could talk to him.

He apologized profusely for not calling before, and he seemed genuinely concerned about my illness. The conversation was difficult because his voice kept fading over the long-distance connection.

"Please, honey, can't you come home?" I pleaded. "I need you so badly."

"I want to, but it would be very difficult. We're shooting up here in the Alps, and the weather has been terrible. I'm in every scene. And now Selznick and Huston are having a big feud, and I don't know what's going to happen."

"But I need you!"

"I know. But I—" His voice faded.

"What? I can't hear you."

"I said I'll try very hard to come home."

At least I had hope, and the hope sustained me for several days.

The news of my illness leaked out, and Louella Parsons wrote this front-page story:

Phyllis Hudson, Rock Hudson's wife, is in St. John's Hospital with hepatitis. Her doctor yesterday telephoned Rock, who is in Italy making *A Farewell to Arms,* and the film star plans to return here by March 25, if not sooner.

Doctors believe Phyllis incurred the hepatitis as a result of the ptomaine poisoning she suffered a few weeks ago when she was in New York with Rock.

Her condition is serious, and she'll have to remain in the hospital a month. She had intended to go to Rome with Rock but was not well enough at the time.

Now it looks as if she won't be able to attend the Academy Awards ceremonies with him. Rock has been nominated as Best Actor in *Giant*.

The news story prompted an outpouring of cards and flowers from friends and studio people. I received one hundred and five bouquets, for all of which I sent thank-you notes later. Once the bouquets were in my room, they had to be destroyed because they might spread infection. Most of the time, I had the nurse show them to me through the window, then I sent them to other rooms. Sister Mary told me: "You are making so many people happy. Some of our patients are here for weeks and never receive flowers."

By the third week I was able to eat a little food. I was slightly yellow, but Dr. Brandsma said my color was good compared to most of his hepatitis patients. I was allowed to get out of bed and take short walks down the corridor two or three times a day. Most of the time I lay in bed staring out the window at the angel Moroni with his horn atop the Mormon church and wondering why Rock didn't come.

I felt helpless in the hospital with Rock so many miles away. I was depressed from the hepatitis and also, as I would realize later, from the confusion in our marriage. I thought Rock cared, but now I didn't think so. What was wrong?

In my fourth week at St. John's, I was permitted visitors. One afternoon Jennifer Jones appeared at my door. She was carrying a wicker bed tray with the side pockets filled with every imaginable kind of Elizabeth Arden cosmetic. Oh, how I needed them to cover my yellow face.

"But I thought you were in Italy," I said.

"David let me come home because my mother is ill," Jennifer explained. "I'm going right back."

"How's Rock?" I asked.

"Fine. Working hard. He's very concerned about you."

"Yes, he sends me roses every few days. I sure wish he could come home, if only for a weekend."

"I'll see what I can do."

I learned later that there had been big problems on *A Farewell to Arms*. The clash of two titans—David Selznick and John Huston—was inevitable. Huston wanted to stick to the Hemingway original, with Rock in a World War I haircut; Selznick accused the director of trying to ruin Rock's sex appeal. They also fought over David's insistence that his wife be the central figure. Huston argued that the man should dominate, as in the book and the 1933 movie with Gary Cooper and Helen Hayes. After one of David's stern memos, Huston walked off the location in the Dolomite mountains, where eighty-five hundred Italian soldiers were ready to restage a World War I battle. Charles Vidor took over from Huston.

Despite the production problems, I couldn't understand why Rock couldn't be released to visit me. I said as much to Henry Willson when he came to visit my hospital room. Henry was totally unsympathetic.

"Look, Phyllis," he argued, "Rock is going to win an Oscar for this picture. If you ruin his concentration by making him come home, then you *really* will be depressed."

After he left, I reflected on what a fool I had been even to mention Rock's coming home. Human feelings meant nothing to Henry. His only concern was how his clients could pour more money into his own pockets.

My last hope was that Selznick would allow Rock to return for the Academy Awards. But no. I was supposed to attend the ceremonies and accept Rock's Oscar for *Giant* if he won. Possibly he and Jimmy Dean canceled each other out in the voting. Yul Brynner was named Best Actor of 1956 for *The King and I*.

David Niven's wife Hjördis came to visit me. She was having some minor surgery at St. John's and she had read that I was there. We struck up a friendship that lasted for years, and I later visited her and David in Europe.

While my physical condition improved, my depression did not. "I'm worried about you, Phyllis," Dr. Brandsma said. "I can cure your hepatitis, but I need help with your depression. I'd like you to talk to a colleague of mine at the Beverly Hills Clinic. Her name is Constance Dubois, and she is a clinical psychologist. I think she can help you."

Dr. Dubois arrived later that day. She was a small woman, middle-aged and unassuming but with intent, probing eyes. First she gave me a series of tests, including a Rorschach. We talked a bit, nothing very serious, and she said she would like her associate, Dr. Jim Rankin, to see me.

Dr. Rankin was a psychiatrist, and he had a very businesslike manner. He started by asking, "How are you feeling, Phyllis?"

"I feel depressed," I admitted.

"Have you thought about suicide?"

"No!" I reached behind me for a pillow and hurled it at him.

Dr. Rankin started to laugh. "With responses like that, you're in better shape than you realize," he said. He walked over and gave my arm a squeeze, winked, and walked toward the door. "Dr. Dubois will be here tomorrow," he said.

Dr. Dubois visited me every day. When she started probing into my marriage, I grew very defensive. I tried to paint the same picture that was presented in the fan magazines. The fun couple deliriously in love. I knew within my heart that if I spoke the truth it would cause me pain. So I held back.

My reluctance was transparent to Dr. Dubois. One day she asked me, "You don't feel very loved, do you, Phyllis?"

I started to cry. Soon I was sobbing. Dr. Dubois had made her breakthrough. From that day, my therapy progressed smoothly.

After four weeks, Dr. Brandsma decided I was well

enough to go home. I said good-bye to the nuns and nurses who had been so kind to me and promised to keep in touch. And I did return to visit them, bringing the See's candy that I knew the nuns loved.

Steve and Pat came to take me home—two cars were needed because of all the flowers and vases. I gave the chrysanthemums to Dr. Dubois, who planted them in her garden. What a thrill to see Demi again, I had missed him terribly. Pat and Steve had waited to tell me about Demi's emergency. He had gotten into the storeroom and drunk some turpentine. Fortunately, Steve and Pat found out, and they rushed him to the veterinarian to have his stomach pumped. Thank God. It would have been terrible if I had come home and found him gone.

Dr. Brandsma arranged for a day nurse, and Steve and Pat took turns staying with me at night. Dr. Dubois came every day during the first week, then she felt I was making good progress and began seeing me three times a week. After a month I felt well enough to dispense with the nurse, and I hired a housekeeper to clean the house and prepare my strict diet. Drinking was verboten, not even a glass of wine, and I was supposed to consume a lot of sugar. I sucked on lemon drops and other hard candies, but after gaining ten pounds I decided to leave them alone. My bruised liver was beginning to heal.

Soon I was able to drive, and I accepted the invitation of Hjördis Niven, who was herself recovering from surgery, to paint with her. I had told her that I loved to paint, and Rock and I had done a few canvases after we were married. I drove out to her home in Pacific Palisades, where she had a little studio. We chatted a bit, but mostly we just painted in blissful silence. Some of her friends, like Betty Bogart and Pat Medina, Joseph Cotten's wife, dropped in to see how Hjördis was recovering. Occasionally David joined us in a painting session. He intimidated us because he was so talented.

I often dined at Kathy and Lou L'Amour's apartment on

Havenhurst. Anna Kashfi, whom I had met when Rock was making *Battle Hymn,* was living behind the L'Amours, and she often joined us. She was strikingly beautiful in an exotic kind of way, and I could see why Marlon Brando was so enamored of her. She had us laughing over some of her adventures with the unpredictable Marlon, and I told of my short acquaintance with him during my early New York days.

Every few weeks, I received a call from Rock, usually on Sunday. He told me all the troubles they were having on *A Farewell to Arms,* and I always asked him, "Can't you come home?" His answer was a standard "I'll try." But the months stretched on, and he never arrived.

Meanwhile the fan magazines carried a different version of our separation. One of the articles told how lonely Rock was.

> For a while he tried to keep busy sight-seeing. It didn't work. Phyllis's absence made even Rome, Italy, seem flat and dull. If he could have shared with her what he saw, it would have been wonderful fun. Alone it was a drag. He did the things he normally would have enjoyed alone—he read books and listened to records. But he couldn't keep his mind on the records or the books. His fears about Phil [sic] would start to close in on him. He wrote long letters to Phil and anxiously waited for calls from her doctor.
>
> Then one night it happened. The call he had prayed for came. It was the doctor. Through the static Rock heard him say, "Phil's better, Rock . . ."
>
> Rock was unable to speak for a moment. Then he murmured his thanks to the doctor and put the receiver down slowly.
>
> The long weeks of gnawing fear and loneliness were over. He would not lose his Phyllis. She would be there, standing in the doorway of their home with her arms stretched out to hold him tight when he made *the long journey home.*

Here is an excerpt from another story, entitled "A Long Way from Home."

. . . He'd always shuddered at the way they put it down in books. The light in the window, the little woman at the door, the roast in the oven, dinner by candlelight, the kiss as you stepped through the door. Somehow, writing to Phyllis, it was easier to express it. "Darling . . . This is what happened today." And in those six words, you managed to sum up a marriage pretty neatly. Someone to talk to. Understanding. Someone to share things with, so you might never be lonely again. Only, somehow letters weren't as good as the real thing. They made you miss a person more.

Very often he'd disappear early and the click of typewriter keys could be heard coming from his room. Some days, he'd walk away from a take and vanish into his dressing room. Photographer Bob Willoughby found him there one day . . .

"Writing to your business manager?" asked Willoughby.

"To my wife," said Rock, "and it should have gotten in the mail yesterday . . ."

I never received a letter from Rock in Italy.

18

Homecoming

"THAT NOISE! How can you stand it?"

Dr. Brandsma was visiting me one afternoon while the carpenters were busily hammering on the frame of the new house next door.

"It *is* pretty bad," I admitted. "And they start at six-thirty in the morning."

"The noise isn't good for you in your condition," he said. "You must get out of here until they finish that house."

The next day I called a realtor friend who said he had just the right place for me. It was a small beach house south of Malibu, and I fell in love the moment I saw it. "I'll take it," I said. I signed a one-year lease.

The house was a little run-down, so I ordered new paint and new carpets in matching light blue-gray. I bought inexpensive furniture, mostly white. I spent a week laying mosaic tile on the kitchen counter, soft gray with white grout; it took hours to get the tiles lined up straight. The house had two levels. The front door faced on Pacific Coast Highway, and it led to the bedroom level—a master suite with ample closets, a smaller bedroom, two baths. Downstairs were a large living room and kitchen, both facing onto the beach and ocean. Outside the living room was a small patio under which the waves would rush at high tide.

In the center of the living room I put a round, low table with four oversize leather pillows for dining. At one end of the room were built-in bookcases where I placed the hi-fi. Most of the furniture was large and comfortable, the fabrics white with light blue accents. Calm and peaceful, just what I needed.

During the first month, a woman stayed with me to do the cooking. I let her go because there were only two bedrooms, and I wanted my friends to be able to stay all night if they liked. Eating was no problem, since there were many good restaurants in Malibu. Hjördis Niven came to paint ocean scenes with me. Anna Kashfi paid a visit. Kathy and Lou L'Amour, Pat and Rux, and Steve Evans all drove to the beach for visits and to keep up my morale.

Most of the time I spent alone with Demi, and what a joyful companion he was. Every day we took our walk together on the beach. He loved exploring this exciting new world, racing after the seagulls, dodging the waves as they crashed on the shore. He seemed to sense my mood, and he was able to cheer me up when I was blue.

I was managing to live with the hurt of Rock's absence. I kept busy decorating the house, painting, reading and writing poems, hundreds of them. I had Demi for company. Sometimes I drove into town and picked up the mail at the Sparrow house and remained overnight. Mostly I stayed at the beach, where the vastness of the ocean helped soothe my bruised spirit.

My twice-a-week visits to Dr. Dubois were also helping

me to recover. While she was probing into my psyche, I learned about her. She had come from Chicago, where her father had been a doctor. She married and gave birth to twins; a girl died immediately, a boy lived. She had divorced, and her grown son was now working in Chicago with her ex-husband. A small woman who was always beautifully groomed, Dr. Dubois had a thorough background in the arts and loved concerts and the theater. An accomplished artist herself, she gave me art books and encouraged me to paint.

Dr. Dubois and I worked hard on my marriage problems, and for the first time I was beginning to see them in a clear light.

The situation was this: I did not feel loved at all. Rock was working very hard as his career reached the heights. But whenever he had free moments, he would leave and spend them with his "other" friends. What was my role in his life? Did I exist solely to have a quick bang and to use as an ornament for premieres and parties and fan mags?

Did I love him? Yes.

Did I feel wanted? No.

"I'll tell you one of your problems," Dr. Dubois said. "You are an adult, but you have to act like a child in order to get along with Rock. You play childish games. You play-act as a movie star's wife, doing things that other people dream of but which are far removed from reality."

"It's true," I admitted. "I can never get Rock to talk about anything serious. Whenever I try to, he thinks he is being criticized, and he withdraws. So I end up speaking to him in baby talk, which is what he and his mother use with each other."

I told Dr. Dubois how frustrated and angry and distraught I became because of Rock's dark moods. I never knew when he would make conversation again. Dr. Dubois rarely made any prognosis, but I could tell she believed I was making progress. At first I blamed myself. As the weeks of treatment continued, I became more analytical.

"We'll work it out," Dr. Dubois assured me. "When Rock gets home, you bring him in and we'll have him work with Dr. Rankin. If Rock will cooperate, there's a good chance we can solve your problems."

HENRY WILLSON was on the telephone. "I'm going to Italy to see Rock, Phyllis. I'll give him your love."

"Why are you going? Won't Rock be home soon?"

"Yes, probably in a couple of weeks. I have a contract for him to sign. It can't wait."

Hmmm. Something smelled fishy. I called one of Henry's other clients, who told me: "Yes, Henry's going to Europe, and he's taking _____ with him." Hmmm again. Why would Henry make an expensive trip to Europe, taking along one of his pretty-boy clients, just to get Rock's signature on a piece of paper?

I did some more sleuthing. Another client, one I knew was on the outs with Henry, told me: "I think Universal is paying for the trip."

Slowly the light dawned. Rock rarely discussed his business affairs with me, but before he left for Italy he said to me, "Sometimes I wonder if Henry is two-timing me; I have a feeling he's selling me short."

Those words came back to me as I contemplated Henry's unusual trip. Was he getting a kickback for delivering Rock at a salary that was below his actual worth?

With a new confidence born out of my sessions with Dr. Dubois, I decided to take action.

Humphrey Bogart had told me that he placed all his business affairs in the hands of the Morgan Maree office, which managed business for many top personalities in Hollywood. I made an appointment with Morgan Maree and explained to him what I knew about Rock's financial situation. Maree told me to bring Rock for a consultation as soon as he returned from Italy. I knew that Henry would be livid over my interference with his control over Rock. I didn't give a damn.

After being gone for five months, Rock finally came home in the last week of July.

The studio sent a limousine to take me from the beach house to the airport. When Rock came through the gate, he looked tan and terrific. He swept me into his arms amid a burst of flashbulbs—Universal had tipped off the press about his arrival.

When we were finally alone in the limo, Rock couldn't have been sweeter. "I missed you so much, Bunting," he said. "It was awful being stuck over there without you." As soon as we arrived at the beach house, he took me to the bedroom and we made love. For the moment I forgot all the hurt and anguish of his absence.

"Now don't you move," he said afterward. "I'm going for a quick swim in the ocean, then I have some surprises to show you."

I felt a warm glow as I watched the beautiful figure race over the sand and dive into the breakers. He really *did* love me in his own peculiar way. This *was* the man I had married, vibrant and charming and incurably romantic. I felt a surge of confidence that all my talks with Dr. Dubois had resulted in a fresh understanding of our relationship. And if Rock would join in the treatment, our marriage would be solid and enduring.

I made a pot of coffee, knowing he would be chilled from the surf. He came in the house dripping. "Man, it's good to be back!" he said. "I don't feel good when you're not with me." I could have said that I hadn't been feeling so hot either, but I didn't.

Rock ran upstairs and brought back two heavy suitcases. He opened them excitedly and started handing me packages. First, a black suede coat lined with striped rabbit fur. "I got this when I was in the Alps," he said. "Feel the fur."

Out of the same suitcase came two wool sweaters, one light blue, one beige, with pearl buttons down the front.

The gifts kept coming. An antique watch, shaped like a man's pocket watch, with a colored cloisonné cover and a small winding key on a chain. A solid gold evening bag. A gold and ivory bracelet. Two pairs of gold cuff links. A gold lipstick case with a matching compact. Four pairs of gold and pearl earrings, all from Buccellati. It took an hour to open all the packages, and longer to admire them.

The happy feeling continued when we went out for dinner. But by the time we returned to the beach house, he seemed depressed and moody again. Jet lag, I thought. Or was I making excuses again?

In the morning I told Rock about my contact with the Morgan Maree office. To my surprise, he approved. I had made an appointment to see Maree that morning, and Rock agreed to go.

Henry telephoned early. He told me he had some riders he wanted Rock to initial on the contract he had taken to Italy. "I'm coming down there this morning," Henry said.

"No, please don't, Henry," I said firmly. "Rock and I are going out this morning. We'll call you later."

"Very well," Henry said with a decided chill in his voice. He hung up.

Rock and I had a successful meeting with Morgan Maree. Rock agreed to place all his business affairs in the hands of the Maree office, though Henry, of course, would remain as his agent. For the first time in our marriage, we would have a joint bank account. I could finally sign checks! I was no longer a non-person.

When Henry was informed of the new arrangement, his reaction was predictable. He was incensed. However, he was careful not to antagonize the champion in his stable. "If that's the way you want it, Rock," he said defensively.

"I think it's better to keep the business part and the agency separated, Henry," Rock said. I was proud of him. It was the first time I had ever heard Rock stand up to Henry. Always it had been "Yes, Henry, whatever you say, Henry."

Henry's Machiavellian mind told him who was responsible for the switch to the Maree office. From that day forward, our relationship changed. Henry had first treated me as his protégée, then as the useful consort of his best client. Now he viewed me as a dangerous monster that he, like a well-meaning Dr. Frankenstein, had created. Henry never dared to insult me; that would have endangered his relations with Rock. He treated me almost as though I didn't exist, which was fine with me. The less I had to do with Henry, the better I felt.

"Rock, I wish you wouldn't see so much of Henry," I said.

"But I *have* to," Rock said. "He's my agent."

"Yes, but why can't you keep it on a businesslike basis? You don't have to see him socially."

"I don't want to hurt his feelings."

"Baloney," I said. "Henry has no feelings."

My efforts to draw Rock away from Henry were unsuccessful. Rock seemed to have an unswerving loyalty to the man who had discovered him, nurtured his career, even provided his professional name. I admired his loyalty, but movie stars had often outgrown their original agents and sought other representation. I firmly believed that Henry Willson was no longer an asset to Rock's career. In fact, I suspected that Henry had been conniving with the producers to rob my husband of the earnings he deserved.

I didn't realize what a formidable enemy I had made. I had done the unforgivable: I had threatened Henry's relationship with Rock. Now Henry was determined to do everything possible to destroy my credibility.

Meanwhile, I was doing everything I could to make our marriage work. I discussed the problems with Dr. Dubois. For one thing, I had to contend with all the pressures from the studio. Rock was constantly on call—go here, go there, do this interview, attend this premiere, accept that award. Rock never said no. He had an inordinate fear that if he refused to do something the studio asked, his whole career would disintegrate.

Then there was the pressure from Henry. He was always

calling to say, "Rock, meet me at Villa Nova, I've got something to show you." Or, "Come down to Scandia, I've got some great news." Usually the call would come during "our time" before dinner. Rock always heeded Henry's summons.

I told Dr. Dubois of many things that bothered me about Rock. His lack of communication—how many times I had said, fruitlessly, "Rock, we must talk about this." His need for the company of people like Mark and George and how childish he seemed with them. His sexual problems. His messiness, the need for someone to clean up after him, as though he were a helpless child. His constant drifting, daydreaming all the time; in the middle of a conversation I would see him simply "go off." His terrible, terrible mood swings.

But there were endearing things about him, too. His sense of humor, simply great. His childlike goodness and eagerness to be loved. His way of demonstrating his love through gifts. His thoughtfulness in things such as the photo album of Demi. How nicely he got along with my friends, Pat, Kathy and Lou, Don and Betsy Weir.

I also told Dr. Dubois about my own insecurities, how uncomfortable I could be around movie people. They seemed so phony to me, always flattering but never seeming to mean it. I never knew what to talk to them about until I found a solution. All I had to do was ask, "How is your movie going?" That was good for an hour's recitation.

I believed that with my self-discovery through the help of Dr. Dubois and with extra effort by Rock and me, our marriage would survive. But shortly after Rock came home, I encountered one of the most painful experiences of my life.

19

Broken Promises

A FEW DAYS after Rock's return from *A Farewell to Arms*, he took me to dinner in Malibu. It was a pleasant evening, almost like old times. We shared a bottle of Pouilly-Fuissé, and I felt renewed optimism that our troubles would be solved—provided Rock would join me in marriage counseling.

When we returned to the beach house, I noticed the balcony gate was ajar. "Rock, didn't you hook the gate?" I asked.

"No, I forgot."

"But I asked you to. You know that Demi can get out if the gate's open."

"I'm sorry. I forgot."

My heart was beginning to pound as I hurried to the front door. Pinned to the door was a note: "Your little dog ran out on the highway and was run over. We have him next door. So sorry."

"Oh, my God!" I screamed. It was too much of a shock, coming after all the troubles of the past five months. Demi had been my best friend during all that time, my constant companion, and, yes, I suppose psychiatrists would say, my baby. No matter how depressed I felt, he could always cheer me with his friendliness and inexhaustible energy.

I became hysterical, sobbing with pain. Rock was miserable too; he loved Demi as much as I did.

"Hit me," he said. "It will make you feel better."

Nothing he could say would console me. I lost control, and I did the one thing Dr. Dubois had asked me not to do: get angry with Rock before she had some time to work with him. Unreasoningly, I poured out all the anger and frustration that had been stored within me for five months.

"You're selfish and mean. I feel sorry for you . . . All you ever think about is your damn career, nothing else is important to you . . . You didn't even care that I was sick. You could have come home from Italy. You just didn't want to . . . I'm tired of your friends; they're silly and shallow, just like little kids."

I couldn't stop sobbing, and Rock realized he was unable to handle the situation. He telephoned Dr. Dubois. I was still hysterical when she arrived. She gave me a tranquilizer and sat on the edge of the bed and talked to me quietly. After a while I fell asleep.

Dr. Dubois went downstairs and stayed for a couple of hours until she was certain that I would continue resting. She tried to console Rock, who was himself shaken emotionally. "I really think for the sake of your marriage that you should come to my office for some testing," said Dr. Dubois.

"I will," Rock promised. "I will."

I was more composed in the morning, but I remained firm. "Let's go see Dr. Dubois today," I said. Rock agreed, and I made an appointment for two o'clock in the afternoon.

Dr. Dubois gave Rock his tests first, the standard ones she had given me in the hospital. Then I spent an hour alone with her, talking mostly about the loss of Demi. I suppose one should not become so attached to a pet, but Demi had provided solace when I needed it most. I had taken him everywhere, carrying him in a large purse that was open at the top. For hours I would sit on the floor and roll a ball for him while I read a book. The thought of his being crushed under a truck was horrifying to me.

Rock tolerated his testing—at least he didn't complain. He was gentle and tender toward me, and he understood when I said I couldn't live in the beach house anymore. Too many memories of Demi. We packed all our beach things and moved back to the Sparrow house.

"This place is too small for us," Rock announced. "I think we should move. I've heard about a place up on Coldwater that would be just right."

Rock drove me up Coldwater Canyon, then he turned on a long driveway that led to the crest of a hill. On top was a beautiful English manor house with a swimming pool in back, surrounded by lovely gardens.

"The property has two acres," Rock said enthusiastically. "Plenty of flat space to build a tennis court."

"It's wonderful, Rock," I said. "How much do they want for it?"

"A hundred and thirty thousand."

My spirits fell. "Oh, dear. A hundred and thirty thousand! I don't see how we can. I think it's too risky, darling." It was one of the less intelligent decisions of my life, as later events would prove.

ROCK AND I WERE HOME one day when the telephone rang. I answered it. "Phyllis, this is Dr. Brandsma. I would like to speak to Rock."

I gave the phone to Rock and went into the bedroom to read a book. Soon afterward Rock rushed into the room and threw himself on the bed. He started to weep.

"Darling, what is it?" I asked. "What did he say? What happened?"

"He wants me to start work with Dr. Rankin. He said I need some help."

I put my arm around him consolingly. "Maybe you should do what Dr. Brandsma says."

"But I can't!"

"Why not?"

"I can't tell anyone what I do when I'm alone."

I was taken aback. "Why? What could you do that's so bad? Masturbate?"

Rock didn't answer. He sobbed and sobbed.

"Honey, look, nothing could be this bad," I said. "Do what Dr. Brandsma suggests. He's your doctor. He knows what's best for you. Do it. I've been under treatment for six months, and I've learned a lot from it. I know it will be difficult, not only for you, but for me too. I may become your hate-figures—your mother, your father. But remember this: Dr. Dubois told me analysis is like shaking up the brain; when you're finished all the pieces will go back in the right places. You'll feel so much better. And even if you don't want me anymore, I will understand. At least you'll be happy. I love you, honey. I think it will be for the best."

Rock's sobs had subsided. "I'll go. I do think I need it. I've never been so confused."

We hugged and kissed, and Rock went into the garden. He spent two hours climbing around the slope, weeding and clipping the ivy; he always said he did his best thinking up there. I tried to read his face. Did he believe what he had told me, that he realized he needed help? I couldn't find the answer.

ROCK WENT TO SEE DR. RANKIN twice in the first week. Each time he came home morose and angry. Oh, dear, I thought, I'm going to have a rough road ahead. He's going to blame me for making him consult Dr. Rankin. All the pain of revelation he'll go through will be my fault. I steeled myself for the worst. If I had to endure weeks, months of torment in order to save my marriage, I would have to make the sacrifice.

I planned an outing that I thought Rock would enjoy. I bought some tickets to the Laguna Festival of the Arts and invited Pat Devlin and Steve Evans to join us. It was a warm August day, and we were all cheerful as we drove south on the freeway in Rock's convertible. We ate a picnic dinner on the beach, watching the golden sun slide into the Pacific. I couldn't drink, but I brought along a couple of our best red wines from the storeroom. Rock consumed one of the bottles by himself.

We walked up Laguna Canyon to the festival grounds and spent an hour looking at the paintings, sculpture, and handicrafts by the Laguna artists. Then we went inside the amphitheater for the Pageant of the Masters. Each year the local residents don makeup and costumes to re-create works of art. The highlight of the show is always "The Last Supper," which is reproduced with amazing fidelity.

Pat, Steve, and I oohed and aahed at every attraction. Rock remained silent. He had brought along the unfinished bottle of wine, and he was drinking from it. With each swallow, his mood grew darker.

He remained silent as we drove northward on the freeway. Embarrassed, I tried to keep up a conversation with Pat and Steve, and they did their best to ignore the situation. I glanced down at the speedometer and was aghast to see we were going eighty miles an hour.

"Slow down, Rock," I said. "Are you trying to do a Jimmy Dean?"

Whap! He backhanded me across the face. "Don't tell me how to drive!" he shouted.

I began screeching. "You bastard! How dare you hit me! What kind of man are you?"

Whap! He hit me again. My mouth was bleeding and I was getting hysterical.

"Rock, stop it!" Pat yelled. "You are being stupid!"

He returned his attention to the freeway in stony silence. I climbed over to the back seat and sat crying between Pat and Steve. Rock never said a word on the way home.

I went to bed immediately, and Pat stayed with me until I went to sleep. Rock and Steve were talking out on the patio. That night, for the first time, Rock slept in the guest bedroom. In the morning he showed no contrition, and I made no reference to what had happened the night before. This is the way it's going to be, I told myself. He's going to aim all his anger and frustration at the nearest target: me. Hold on, Phyllis, I kept saying. It isn't going to be easy.

Rock kept one more appointment with Dr. Rankin. He came home and said, "Dr. Rankin is a Milquetoast. I'm not going to see him any longer."

So I had failed. Rock's reaction was typical, doctors have told me; when patients fear the doctor is breaking through their armor, they quit, disparaging the doctor.

I sometimes contemplate what might have happened if Rock had continued his treatment by Dr. Rankin. Would it have saved our marriage? Probably not. Would it have changed his lifestyle? I doubt it. But at least Rock might have learned to understand himself and perhaps avoid the torment of his later years.

ROCK WAS INVOLVED with looping (re-recording dialogue) for *A Farewell to Arms,* and he gave the usual interviews, telling eager fan mag writers what a wonderful marriage he had. When he came home, his moods were horrendous. He rarely spoke to me unless he had to. Still, he wanted me to go with him on the Hawaiian locations for his next movie, *Twilight for the Gods*. I was reluctant. Why travel three thousand miles to be miserable?

"I think you should go, Phyllis," Dr. Dubois said. "I know you're not feeling well, but please try. If there is any chance of saving your marriage, you must find out."

Since the death of Demi, I was seeing Dr. Dubois every day, trying desperately to sort out the confusion and hurt I was feeling.

"I can't understand why Rock hasn't kept his appointments with Dr. Rankin," Dr. Dubois said. "He has broken six."

"He doesn't *want* to help himself, Dr. Dubois," I said. "Every day he is around people who tell him how perfect he is."

"Rock is a very depressed human being, Phyllis. He doesn't know *who* he is anymore. If only he would leave that dreadful agent of his."

If only. Henry Willson had declared war on me ever since I convinced Rock to switch his business matters to the Morgan Maree office. Henry lived in mortal terror that I would persuade Rock to change agents. Henry was about to launch a campaign to destroy me and my marriage, spreading venom to everyone he could.

"Henry is telling people you are cheating on Rock," my close friend John Smith told me.

I was horrified. "How dare he!"

"I told him he was a liar. I said I knew you too well. But that won't stop him. Henry will be vicious about anyone who crosses him. He'll stop at nothing."

Well, I thought, I can be tough too. But I didn't realize what a formidable opponent I was facing, nor the iron grip that Henry had on Rock. Henry would resort to anything to keep from losing Rock, even blackmail.

20

Aloha

SEPTEMBER, 1957. After the endless blue of the Pacific, suddenly the volcanic islands rose out of the ocean, and we were passing over Hawaii. I recognized the stolid profile of Diamond Head, then saw the string of hotels on Waikiki—no high-rises yet. We flew over Pearl Harbor, and Rock pointed out to me the USS *Arizona* in its shallow grave.

I was feeling better, and the embracing tropical warmth added to my well-being. Rock had been more like his former self in the days before our departure. He always had a sense of elation before starting a new movie.

A representative of Universal met us at the airport and took us in a limousine to the Royal Hawaiian Hotel, where we were shown to a lovely suite. The director of *Twilight for the Gods,* Joe Pevney, came up for a drink and offered to take us to dinner.

"No, thanks, Joe," Rock said. "Phyllis and I want to be alone tonight."

It was a small gesture, but I was thrilled by it. We ate by candlelight at Chuck's Steak House, then went back to the hotel and danced outside to the languorous strains of the Hawaiian orchestra, leis of carnation and plumeria around our necks. Rock was as attentive and tender as he had been on our honeymoon in Jamaica.

Both of us were a little on guard, fearful of shattering the romance of the moment. Rock was unusually reflective.

"I think maybe I have been too absorbed with my career," he said. "I've never thought about anything else. Have I been selfish?"

Should I lie and try to please him? No, I thought, I've done that for too long.

"Yes," I replied. "You have."

"I wish I could change. I'm gonna try. Honest to God, I'm gonna try."

IN THE MORNING we flew to the island of Maui. Our hotel was built in island style, sprawling and open, every room with a lanai filled with hibiscus plants and other flowering shrubs. We arrived at lunchtime, and Joe Pevney escorted us around the dining room to meet members of the company—Cyd Charisse, Arthur Kennedy, Leif Erickson, Charles McGraw, and others. The food was bountiful—platters of shrimp and crab salads, pineapple, mango, papaya, kiwi, bananas, etc.

I felt as if in a trance in Hawaii. Still weakened by hepatitis, I floated through the days, desiring nothing but rest. Occasionally I could be induced to partake of the diversions. I rode with some of the other location wives to see the smoldering volcanoes. I took a catamaran ride, and the cameraman's wife convinced me to try some hula lessons. I drove one day to the black beach. But such outings tired me quickly, and I could hardly wait to get back to the hotel room and lie down.

Cyd Charisse became a good friend. She was always pleasant and cheerful, even though she was apart from her husband, Tony Martin, who was singing in Las Vegas. I often ate with Cyd and her stand-in, and we had many laughs together. One night Cyd was especially sad after talking to Tony on the telephone. Rock and I bought a bouquet of anthuriums, the "male" flower, and taped them to Cyd's door with a note: "We know how you miss Tony."

Before I had left California, I had spent some time with Anna Kashfi. She was going through a turbulent time with Marlon Brando, and I convinced both of them to consult with Dr. Dubois. Their relationship was complicated further when Anna discovered she was pregnant. Anna wanted to get married; Marlon was reluctant to commit himself to any attachment.

On October 11, Anna telephoned me from the mainland with the happy news: she and Marlon had just been married. They were going to spend their honeymoon with Kathy and Louie L'Amour in La Quinta. "Have a glass of champagne for us," Anna said buoyantly.

I couldn't drink champagne, or anything else alcoholic, but I did make a mental toast to Anna and Marlon, hoping they could find happiness with themselves and their baby. I was running low on any such hope for Rock and me.

Things really hadn't changed between us. Whenever Rock had time off from the location, he went scuba diving instead of spending time with me. A couple of times I asked him about seeing Dr. Rankin, and he cut me off immediately. I couldn't breach the barrier. He seemed depressed and yet he laughed much of the time, that deep laugh that entranced everyone. Only I could tell that it was hollow.

AS SOON AS WE RETURNED from Hawaii, I made an appointment with Dr. Dubois. I told her the trip had been unsuccessful, as far as bridging the gap between Rock and me. We didn't even make love during the entire two weeks.

"I don't know what is wrong, Dr. Dubois," I said dejectedly. "I can't seem to reach Rock. He has shut me off from him."

"You're the one who has been sick, Phyllis," she replied. "I don't know how much more of this anguish you can take. You must start thinking of yourself."

"But what can I do?"

"Perhaps it is time for a showdown. Ask him once and for all, will he see Dr. Rankin?"

When I returned home, Rock was up on the slope, clipping ivy in his work clothes. "When are you going to see Dr. Rankin?" I asked.

His face became steely. "Never!" he said. "He is a Milquetoast, and I never want to see him."

He was being like a little child, stamping his foot and saying he wouldn't take his medicine. But then, I realized, he had always lived in a child's world. His mother had pampered and babied him; she still talked to him as if he were a child. He had become an actor: more make-believe. As a movie star, his every wish was catered to. He took no responsibility on himself; everything was done for him. He didn't even pay his own bills.

Henry Willson had become like an evil father to Rock, manipulating him, guiding his personal and professional lives in ways that would further the desires of Henry Willson. Henry demanded complete control over Rock, and I, Phyllis Hudson, was his stumbling block. I was the enemy. I'm sure that Henry was telling Rock: "Where the hell does she get off telling you to see a shrink? *She's* the one who had to go to the hospital. Hepatitis, they called it. I think she's off her rocker."

I visited Dr. Dubois again the next day. I told her of my continuing impasse with Rock. She looked at me with her kind, deep eyes and said, "I think you're very close to having a nervous breakdown." She paused, then added, "Phyllis, aren't you tired of being a doormat?"

I came home for the one-sided conversations between myself and Rock, who was usually hiding under the covers. I couldn't help being amused by the note he left when he finally left: "I'm going to the Beverly Hills Hotel. Let's keep it quiet." He wants to keep the separation secret and he checks into the Beverly Hills Hotel!

It was hardly a surprise to me the next morning when I read Louella Parsons's story on the front page of the Los Angeles *Examiner:*

> One of the biggest surprises to hit Hollywood in a long time came yesterday when Rock Hudson moved into the Beverly Hills Hotel under an assumed name.
>
> His wife Phyllis remained at the family home. Neither intends to make an official statement, but there can be no denial of the fact that the Hudsons' marriage has hit a snag.
>
> Their friends believe that this might be one of those things that happen in the best of Hollywood families—an argument and then the kiss-and-make-up reconciliation.
>
> Rock and Phyllis had just returned from Hawaii, where he had been filming location scenes for "Twilight for the Gods." They seemed very happy there, and there was no hint of trouble.
>
> But previous to this they had been separated by distance for five months. Rock had been making "A Farewell to Arms" for David Selznick in Italy, and Phyllis had not been able to join him because she was seriously ill with hepatitis.
>
> However, Rock called her daily on the telephone from Italy . . .

Friends began calling. They asked me to have dinner with them. I declined. I was afraid I might break into tears in the middle of dinner. Besides, if I left the house, I might miss a call from Rock.

Everyone who called had an observation to make. "You'll be better off." I didn't think so. "He'll come back." He didn't call. "You can build a new life for yourself." What life? Being a movie star's wife doesn't train you for anything else.

I visited Dr. Dubois every day, laden with self-pity. She told me: "There's nothing you can do. It's out of your hands. You tried everything you could. If he won't help himself, you can't help him."

I was hurt and confused. I couldn't eat, I couldn't sleep. Dr. Brandsma came to the house and brought some tranquilizers. "You must not make yourself sick over this," he said.

I told him what Dr. Dubois had said.

"She's absolutely right," he said. "You can't hope any longer. There's no chance if he won't seek help. Get on with your life. You're a beautiful woman. All kinds of doors will open for you."

I listened, but I didn't hear. My mind was still fixed on that phone call from Rock. Every time I heard the telephone ring, I jumped. But the caller was never Rock. Four days after we separated, I received an invitation, engraved in gold:

Rock Hudson
would appreciate your company for dinner
on the evening of November 3, 1957
I will pick you up promptly
at 7 o'clock
Is the Beachcomber's okay?
Rock

I spent half the afternoon in the beauty parlor, and I dressed as excitedly as a girl on a prom date. Rock never looked handsomer than when he arrived at the front door. We drove into Hollywood and went to our favorite booth in Don the Beachcomber's, which served the best Polynesian food in town. The Mai Tais helped ease the conversation, and we talked for an hour about a variety of things, mostly trivial. Then Rock said, "Can we get back together?"

"I love you with all my heart, Rock," I said. "But we have

problems. I don't think they will ever be resolved unless you see Dr. Rankin."

He quickly looked away. "I don't want to see Dr. Rankin," he said.

"Then I can't see our relationship going anywhere. The only thing that can help us is analysis. It can be painful, but the reward of self-discovery is worth the price. It's the most wonderful experience I've ever had."

Rock displayed a glimmer of interest. "How does it work?"

"Dr. Dubois explains it like this: The doctor holds your hand until you are capable of extending your hand to others."

A tear ran down Rock's face. "I just can't do it. I can't tell anyone all about myself."

"You could! To a doctor, Rock, you're not an unusual case. You just think you are. Everyone has problems. Believe me, doctors like Dubois and Rankin have heard everything."

Rock's face was filled with anxiety, and for a moment I thought he would relent. "I'll be there to help you," I said. "You can't imagine how wonderful you will feel when you finish. You'll feel happy and confident, ready to face anything."

He wouldn't commit himself, and the evening ended with our usual impasse.

Rock telephoned me on our anniversary, November 9. We exchanged rueful congratulations, and Rock invited me to the premiere of *A Farewell to Arms* on December 18. "I don't think so," I said.

He called again in the middle of the month and asked again about the premiere. I said I wouldn't feel right about going. I telephoned him on November 17 to wish him a happy birthday. "Henry is taking me to dinner," Rock said.

I felt like saying something nasty about Henry, but I simply replied, "That's nice. Then you won't be alone."

Rock forgot my birthday, December 7, but he called a few days later, again to ask about the premiere. How ironical, I thought. He can't remember my birthday, but he still wants me as window dressing for his career. "Henry told me to ask you," he said.

"If Henry is so interested, why doesn't *he* call me?"

Henry did. In an icy voice he said, "Phyllis, this picture is very important to Rock. He is magnificent in it, better than *Giant*. I *know* he can get the Academy Award for it. We need some upbeat publicity. Having you at his side for the premiere will do it."

"Henry, I'm tired of being used to promote Rock's career. I've been through hell in the past year, and neither you nor Rock gives a damn."

"Then you refuse?"

"I'm not going, no."

"I knew it! I knew you'd try to fuck us up. You bitch!"

I couldn't resist the cliché. "Well, Henry, it takes one to know one."

21

Revelation

THERE HE WAS on television, standing between Jennifer Jones and David Selznick at the premiere of *A Farewell to Arms*. He looked great in his tuxedo, though thinner. Was he suffering too? I wondered. Of course not. He radiated charm, as he always did in public.

I could have been there at his side, clutching his arm, smiling amid the lightning flash of photographers' bulbs. Should I have relented and played Mrs. Rock Hudson one more time? No, that would merely have prolonged the agony of seeing him storm out of the house and arrive back late at night.

After the separation, my life underwent a serious disruption. My own friends remained loyal—Pat Devlin, Steve Evans, Kathy and Louie L'Amour, Carol Lee Anderson, Hjördis Niven. But communication with most of my new-found Hollywood friends ended abruptly with Louella Parsons's disclosure of our separation. It seemed as if a wall descended, separating me from Rock's world.

Cyd Charisse was an exception. She called and invited me to dinner. "I was surprised to read about you and Rock separating," she said. "You and he seemed to have a better relationship than most people in Hollywood. At least you enjoyed each other's company." I thought, what a performance Rock and I must have given in Hawaii! We were so accustomed to going through the routine of a happy marriage that nobody recognized that we were desperately unhappy.

The Martins lived off Coldwater Canyon, not far from the dream house that Rock had proposed we buy. Cyd showed me through her home, which was spacious and in excellent taste. She had a large dressing room that I envied and a marble bathroom with a tub you had to step up to. Cyd had invited two other couples, including her stand-in and her musician husband.

Tony, dressed informally in slacks and an alpaca sweater, mixed drinks in the bar. "I'm sorry about you and Rock," he said.

"So am I," I admitted.

"Do you think you will get back together?"

"I don't know. I would like to, but we have problems we must work out first."

"Nobody stays married in this town. Too much gossip, too much pressure."

I was surprised that during the evening Tony kept calling his wife Tula. I asked him about it. "Didn't you know that Tula Finklea is Cyd's real name?" he said.

Sydney Guilaroff, the hair designer for the stars, invited me to a Christmas party. But I didn't really know him, and I didn't go. I was close to tears at all times, and I didn't want to embarrass myself in public.

I continued seeing Dr. Dubois regularly. I kept asking

her, "Has Rock called Dr. Rankin?" The answer was always negative.

"I'm sure Henry is telling him not to go," I suggested.

"Probably," she said. "He doesn't want to share Rock with anyone."

I saw a few of my friends at dinner. Rock was never mentioned, partly because they knew I didn't want to talk about him, partly because they realized I would break into tears if I did. Dr. Brandsma came by to check on my condition. We drank tea and chatted, but he never told me anything about Rock, not yet. None of my friends disclosed anything about Rock, either. It was a natural tendency to refrain from criticism, on the chance that we might reconcile and I would resent what was said.

Anna Kashfi Brando and I sometimes had lunch together. She was already experiencing problems with Marlon. "He's never home," she complained. I wondered, is that how it works in Hollywood? Once you are married, your husband considers the house merely a place to sleep? What a pretense it was. Why bother to get married at all?

Rock, I concluded, wanted to be married and yet live like a bachelor. He wanted to answer to no one, to come and go as he wished. What kind of a marriage was that?

I had never tried to possess him. I believed that everyone should have a free spirit. There had been times, I admitted, when I was jealous of all the attention he received. But I tried not to show it, and it wasn't all that bad, anyway. I received attention myself, and not simply because I was Mrs. Rock Hudson. Several men found me attractive enough to propose an affair, something that I would *never* entertain. I had always been taught that a wife remained loyal to her husband and that the husband should do the same.

One night during our early marriage, after Rock and I had drunk much wine and made love, he suggested, "Why don't we have someone join us in bed?" I couldn't take him seriously. "What—me, a former Sunday school teacher!" I said. Later I thought, what a terrible thing to say. Did he really mean to share our love with someone else? I thought about his remark for days. It shocked me.

THE DEVLINS INVITED ME to a Christmas Eve dinner, and it was a joyful party sparked by Pat's father, Mickey, and her mother, Maggie. I realized they were trying extra hard to keep me cheered up, and I blessed them for it. But I still couldn't get in the spirit, and I left early so they could open their presents, which occupied half the living room. I attended a candlelight service at a Lutheran church and went back to my lonely house.

Pat's father invited me to an afternoon Christmas dinner at the Bel Air Country Club. I had been asked to a few Christmas parties, but I didn't feel like going. Hjördis Niven told me she saw Rock at one of them. He told her, "I'm so lonely without Phyllis. I don't know why we separated." Always straightforward, Hjördis replied, "Well, if you're so lonely, why don't you go back to her?"

A few days after Christmas, a friend of mine called and suggested having lunch together. He thought it would do me good, and I agreed. Over lunch we talked about the separation, and I said, "I'm certain of one thing: Rock was always loyal to me."

The friend laughed. "Phyllis, Phyllis," he said, "how can you be so naïve?"

"What do you mean?"

"It is common knowledge that Rock was *not* faithful to you."

I looked at him in disbelief. "You're just saying that because you never liked Rock."

"No. That has nothing to do with it. I know, Phyllis, I know. Several people who know him well have told me. Rock was *not* faithful. I never told you because I didn't want you to be hurt. But the marriage is over now, *kaput*. I think it is time for you to wake up."

I was deeply disturbed by what he had told me. I trusted him. He was not one of that Hollywood type who delights in spreading malicious gossip. What he said must have been true. My mind raced. If Rock had been cheating on me, with whom? Elizabeth Taylor? There had been all those rumors of a fling between her and Rock in Texas. I always noticed a certain intimacy between them. It could have been anybody—many people. Actresses, secretaries, producers' wives, stand-ins, fans. A movie star has chances for dalliance every day.

For New Year's Eve, I bought some cold cuts at Nate and Al's and invited Pat Devlin and Steve Evans for sandwiches and champagne. I told Steve of my conversation two days before and asked him if he had heard any stories about Rock.

"Yes, I have," he admitted. "I've heard stories, but I don't know if they are true, and I don't think you should hear them anyway. They might just be gossip."

Dr. Brandsma called. He had been to a party and asked if he could join us "Certainly," I said. The four of us toasted the New Year and tried to maintain an air of gaiety. In my case, it didn't succeed. My only consolation was that 1958 couldn't be worse than 1957. Or could it?

DURING THE FIRST WEEK of January, I realized I hadn't heard from Rock for over a month. There was no telling what devilish schemes Henry might be pushing Rock into. I had certain rights as a spouse, and I had better protect them. I needed a lawyer. But who? I didn't know any Hollywood lawyers, except a few social types I had met at parties. I decided to do what others had done in times of trouble: Get Giesler.

Jerry Giesler was the most famous lawyer in Hollywood, perhaps in America. When Errol Flynn was charged with raping two teenage girls aboard a yacht, Giesler got him off. When Charlie Chaplin was accused of transporting a young woman across state lines for illicit purposes, Giesler won an acquittal. Jerry Giesler was the fatherly figure who stood beside Marilyn Monroe on the lawn of her house and told the press that she was separating from Joe DiMaggio.

I made an appointment to see Mr. Giesler on January 15. His office was in his Beverly Hills home, and I drove up the circular driveway toward an imposing mansion. His secretary greeted me at the door and ushered me into his office.

The office was larger than my living room. It was decorated in shades of brown and beige, with a long desk piled with papers and legal pads, two large brown leather chairs at each side. The wall behind the desk was filled with law books; so was a French country armoire in one corner.

Mr. Giesler was seated on a sofa, holding a cup of coffee. He beckoned for me to sit beside him. He was a large man, somewhat portly, with a ruddy complexion, bald head, and kind eyes. From his reputation, I had expected a dynamic, fast-talking man. He was nothing like that. He spoke in a low, firm voice, like a favorite uncle.

"Would you like a cup of coffee, my dear?" he asked.

"No, thank you," I replied. "I've had too many this morning."

"So you want to get a divorce?"

"Yes," I said hesitantly, my eyes filling with tears.

"Divorces are a very difficult thing to go through," he said. "I always ask my clients if they are certain that's what they want. Are you certain that you have tried everything?"

I poured out the story. How I tried to communicate with Rock but failed. How he virtually abandoned me for five months when I was desperately ill. How he refused counseling to save the marriage. How he left me alone for long periods or else locked himself in the workroom and edited his home movies until early morning. How he would pick fights over trivial matters, then slam the door and return in the middle of the night. He never explained where he had been.

"I still love my husband, Mr. Giesler," I said, "but I can only conclude that he no longer loves me."

Mr. Giesler seemed deep in thought as I recounted my grievances, and I began to wonder if he had been listening. When I finished, he was silent for a moment. Then he spoke.

"Something happened a week before you and Rock married," he said. "Rock and Henry Willson came to see me. They sat right over there in those two chairs by the desk. Henry told me that *Confidential* magazine was planning to run a story that would be very damaging to Rock's career, might even destroy it. I asked what the story was about, and Henry reluctantly told me. It seems there had been a gang bang at Henry's house involving Rock and other young men. One of them talked to *Confidential* about it."

I couldn't believe what I was hearing. I started to perspire, and I felt light-headed. Mr. Giesler called for his secretary to bring a glass of water. "You're very pale, Phyllis," he said. "Here, drink this."

He continued with the story: "Henry and Rock asked me what I could do to stop the story. I told them there was nothing I could do. The First Amendment prohibited prior restraint. Only after the story had been published could they sue for damages. Both men were very disappointed by what I told them. On their way out, I heard Henry say, 'We've *got* to find a way!' I didn't know what he meant. Now I do."

Mr. Giesler said he would begin the procedures for the divorce. He seemed gravely concerned for my well-being, and he advised me to get plenty of rest and to be careful. I wasn't certain what he meant about being careful.

Driving home, I tried to grasp the enormity of what he had told me. The whole thing was too nightmarish to comprehend.

Was Rock a homosexual? I couldn't believe that. He had always been the manliest of men. Though our lovemaking had often been brief, we had also known moments of sexual passion.

Had our marriage been a cover-up for Rock's true nature? Impossible. I *knew* that Rock had loved me, during the courtship and in the early stages of our marriage.

I needed some answers, and only Rock could give them. The Maree office gave me the number of his new apartment, and I asked him to come by the house that evening. "Sure, I'll be there at six-thirty," he said.

He arrived looking the same—jeans, plaid shirt, and moccasins. We chatted about nothing for a few minutes. Then I told him I had consulted Jerry Giesler. Rock looked quite surprised.

"He told me something very disturbing," I said. "He told me you and Henry had been to his office a week before we got married and asked if he could stop a story that was coming out in *Confidential.*"

Rock's face whitened. "Did he tell you what the story was about?" he asked.

"Yes." I paused. "Is that why you married me, Rock?"

"No, of course not! I didn't marry you because of the *Confidential* story. We got it fixed. We hired a gangst—"

He stopped himself, and he seemed in a panic. "Excuse me, I have to go to the bathroom," he blurted, and he hurried out of the room. I contemplated the import of what he had partially revealed. Had Henry been desperate enough to hire a hoodlum to dissuade the *Confidential* editor from publishing the exposé? I knew that Henry was capable of such a thing; he would fight like a tigress to protect his prized client. But I couldn't imagine that Rock would allow himself to be dragged into such a sordid affair. Or would he? In the past few weeks I had learned so many things about Rock that shocked and surprised me.

When Rock returned, he still seemed shaken.

"Rock, I think it is time for us to talk," I said. "I deserve some explanations. You have been acting strange for the past year. What is going on?"

"Nothing is 'going on,'" he insisted.

"Did you and Henry have an affair?"

"Yes. But it was nothing." He shrugged. "Henry sleeps with most of his clients."

I was too shocked to respond. Until that moment, something within me had tried desperately to discount all the evidence that Rock had been involved in homosexual affairs. Now I had heard it from Rock himself.

While I was trying to grasp the enormity of what I had heard, Rock seized the opportunity and rose. "I have to go," he said nervously. "Henry and I are having dinner with Henry King. He's going to direct my next picture."

He was gone. I had a thousand questions I wanted answered, but I knew it was impossible. Rock would never tell me. He had already told me too much.

I related the conversation to Jerry Giesler the next day. His face clouded. "Phyllis, I don't want you staying home alone at night," he said.

"Why not?" I asked.

"These are ruthless men. There's no telling what they might do."

"But what could they do to me?"

"They could break into your house, force you into a compromising position, take photographs. Believe me when I tell you I have seen it happen in divorce cases. You can stay at the house during the day, not at night."

I was thoroughly frightened. When I told Kathy L'Amour what he had said, she told me, "Then you must stay with us. You can sleep in the guest bedroom every night." I had planned to stay in a small hotel, but I realized that would be even more dangerous. I gratefully accepted her offer. For five months I slept every night in the twin bed of her and Lou's guest bedroom. Wherever I went, I carried my little green overnight case containing my nightgown and toothbrush in my car.

With Dr. Dubois's help I retained my sanity. But I still couldn't comprehend the revelations that had shattered my life. The greatest blow was still to come.

22

The Italian Affair

"YOUR HUSBAND was unfaithful to you in Italy."

"What? I can't believe it."

"It's true. I have proof."

"Who was she?"

"Phyllis, you're so naïve. It wasn't a she. It was a *he.*"

One of my closest friends was telling me this. I had no reason to doubt him. He was not a common gossip, nor was he trying to seek favor with me. He knew the distress I had been through, was still enduring, and he thought he could help.

He had heard about an Italian actor who had arrived in Hollywood, a young man with striking handsomeness. The actor had been Rock's lover in Italy and had flown here to continue the romance. But Rock wouldn't see him, and the

Italian was bitter. My friend invited him for drinks. The Italian spoke openly.

My friend told me that the Italian admitted that he and Rock had been lovers during the entire filming of *A Farewell to Arms*. What's more, the Italian said, Rock had stayed in Rome after filming ended so that they could be together. What hurt me most was to learn that the Italian had been with Rock when Rock telephoned me and professed how much he missed me. Also that the young man had helped Rock select the presents for me.

The Italian had followed Rock to California but now Rock wouldn't see him. "His agent called and told me to leave town," the Italian complained to my friend. "Can you believe that? We were lovers for five months and now he won't see me."

I listened to my friend with tears in my eyes. "Now do you believe?" he asked. I nodded slowly.

"Henry obviously knew about this guy, because he had dinner with the lovers in Rome," he continued. "So Henry is using the affair to blackmail Rock so he won't leave for another agent. But Henry is also scared that the Italian might talk to the press and ruin Rock's career. So he's trying to convince the guy to leave town. If that fails, there's no telling what Henry might do."

"What a bunch of creeps," I said. "What a bunch of liars and users. Rock was trying to reconcile with me because he thought a divorce would hurt his career."

"I'll testify for you, Phyllis. Or you can subpoena the Italian and put him on the stand."

"Not yet. I need to talk to Jerry Giesler. I need to think."

That was the day I realized that most of my feelings for Rock were gone.

I went to see Mr. Giesler the next day and told him what I had learned. "This is a very grave matter," he told me. "It would mean the end of Rock's career. Do you want to use it in your divorce?"

"I don't know," I said. "Right now I'm so hurt and angry

that I can't think. I do know one thing for sure: I don't want him anymore. I don't want to see him. I want nothing to do with him. Do what you have to do. Just get me a divorce."

I telephoned the Morgan Maree office when I got home and was told Rock had rented a beach house. I called a moving company. I had the movers take all of Rock's belongings to his house. I tried to be fair in selecting the things I thought he would like. The oversize bed. The massive bedroom furniture. All of Rock's clothes. The television set he had received for doing the "I Love Lucy" show and the cabinet he had had built for it. His record player and all his records. The baby grand piano I had given him. The antique lamps marked "brandy" and "bourbon." Four silver-plated wine coolers he had received as awards. All of his other awards and photographs, his movie equipment, and more. .

I called Catherine Armstrong and told her I wanted the house redecorated. She and Bill Kipka made it over in shades of white and cranberry. Everything was painted soft pink in my bedroom, including the shutters and closets. The small bedroom was converted to a den. With all that huge furniture gone, the house seemed much bigger.

One day Jerry Giesler called me with the information that Rock's attorney had shut off all my charge accounts. Mr. Giesler had managed to arrange a thousand dollars a month for separate maintenance, but he was so angry about the charge account cutoff that he gave the story to the press.

On the morning that the story appeared in the newspapers, I heard a knock at the door. It was Marlon Brando.

"I read in the paper what they did to you," he said. "What rotten people! Here, take this."

He handed me a thousand-dollar check. I didn't know what to say. "Would you like some coffee?" I asked.

"No, thanks, I have an appointment. But I want you to know that you are welcome to visit Anna and me any time you want. You can come every night for dinner. We have a cook."

I gave him a little kiss on the cheek, and he left. What a warm, compassionate man, I thought. I carried the check with me for a couple of weeks and then left it at his house.

Shortly after Mr. Giesler notified Rock's attorney that I was proceeding with the divorce, I noticed a green Nova following me. Everywhere I went, to the cleaners, the grocery store, Kathy and Lou's for the night, the green Nova was behind me. How stupid, I thought. How boring for the poor detective. He followed me for two months, and a couple of times I even waved to him.

Dr. Dubois had urged me to buy a German shepherd, so I went to a kennel and brought home Gretchen, who was totally black and completely sweet. Too sweet to be a guard dog. At the first sound of thunder, she crawled under the bed. Still, it was a comfort to find her standing by the front door when I arrived home in the morning. We had breakfast together.

One night I was having dinner at home with Anna Brando and Steve Evans when I saw a face at the window. I screamed, and the man and his camera disappeared.

Twice I had threatening phone calls. The message: "If you hurt Rock, something will happen to you." Were they real threats or simply the work of devoted fans? I couldn't tell.

These were bad times for me. I worried constantly about physical danger. I knew that Henry could be vicious; there might be no limit to which he would go to protect his client. Fortunately, he did not yet know that I was aware of Rock's Italian lover. But Rock had undoubtedly admitted his slip: "We hired a gangst—" That might have been enough to incite Henry to do something drastic.

Beyond the danger, I felt a devastating malaise. A thousand questions darted through my mind. Why did Rock do this to me? Why had he hurt me so? Did he ever love me? Did he ever tell me the truth?

How many times had he lied? When friends told me they had seen him in Santa Monica or Westwood, he said, "They must have seen someone else; I was at the studio." Where was he? What was he doing?

So often he would call in the late afternoon and say, "Honey, I'm in the middle of an interview, so I may be late." Then he would call again, and again, until he would miss dinner. But why would he call me during interviews when he never called me during the day? Did he want to convince the interviewer that he was a devoted husband?

After he had finished *Something of Value*, he stopped over in New York. Why? He said he had business matters, but Henry handled all his business matters. Did he need an excursion to the baths?

What about those nights when he slammed the door and disappeared until the early hours of the morning? He never told me where he had been. Was he hanging out in homosexual bars?

Why had Rock first suggested, undoubtedly at Henry's behest, that we get married on a boat off Nassau? Later I learned that the wedding on shipboard would have been illegal; it was a trick that a Broadway producer had pulled on one of his wives. Had Henry and Rock planned a phony wedding so the marriage could be later dissolved with no great financial loss? Only because I had insisted on a Lutheran wedding did we get married in Santa Barbara.

So many questions. No answers.

I felt betrayed, tricked, humiliated. How naïve I had been—a Minnesota farm girl. The big-city sharpsters had played a monstrous game with my feelings. I wanted to be out of it, fast.

"I'm not going to use the Italian actor as corespondent," I told Jerry Giesler. "That would only harm Rock's career, and I'm not going to do that. I just want a divorce, and to be rid of him. I can't take any more lies."

"I'll try to hurry things along, Phyllis," he said. "But Rock's attorney is out of town. It's a game lawyers play."

So I had to wait while the lawyers performed their ministrations. Meanwhile Henry had launched his propaganda campaign against me. He was telling everyone who would listen that I had been an unfaithful wife, that I had amassed huge bills on my charge accounts, hence they had to be cut off. Henry fed the misinformation to the fan magazine writers, and they had a field day analyzing what went wrong with Rock Hudson's perfect marriage.

It seemed that every day I was learning new and startling things about Rock and Henry. I discovered that Henry had used me for his underhanded purposes even before I met Rock.

Remember Bill McGiver, the good-looking blond who drove me to Minnesota in Rock's Lincoln convertible and who later was dropped from the Willson client list? The whole thing had been one of Henry's elaborate Machiavellian plots.

Another Willson client told me the story. Bill shared a house with Rock, and the two men were intimate. Too intimate, Henry believed. He wanted no one else to wield an influence over Rock, and so he set out to poison the relationship. He persuaded Bill to borrow Rock's car for a trip to the Midwest, and then he enlisted me to accompany Bill. When Rock returned from Ireland, he was so incensed over the misuse of his car that he threw Bill out. Henry then dropped Bill as a client and spread lies that guaranteed Bill would never find work in Hollywood. Bill McGiver (that's not his real name) disappeared from sight. But not before he turned up one night at Rock's house—the time I hid in the bedroom—to ask Rock for money.

Rock never mentioned the trip to me, nor did he seem to resent my having gone along. I guess he figured I had nothing to worry about with Bill.

THE MONTHS WORE ON as the lawyers conducted their invisible machinations. With Dr. Dubois's help, I was beginning to arrange my life in a semblance of order. During the summer I spent a lot of time with my neighbors down the hill, Don and Betsy Weir. Their family was a joy to be with because they had five children, the same as my family. I played basketball with them on their lawn, and the kids loved to come up to my house and play with Gretchen. Almost every Sunday morning, Betsy called to say, "The Weirs are serving breakfast on the patio," and I joined them.

I saw Pat and Rux, Kathy and Lou L'Amour, and I often visited Anna Brando and her young son Devi. Marlon was seldom home. One time when he was there, he stared at me intently and said, "You remind me of my mother."

"Is that good or bad?" I asked.

"I'm not going to tell you," he replied.

Dr. Dubois kept urging me to go to college. "It will help you build a new life," she said. She was persuasive, but I realized I would need to improve my grammar and spelling. So I enrolled in a basic English class at UCLA.

I found it hard to concentrate on studies as long as my life was in limbo. Why couldn't the attorneys get things settled so I could start to live again? Every time I called Jerry Giesler, he sounded just as exasperated as I was. "I don't know why they're stalling, Phyllis," he told me, "but there's nothing we can do about it."

Then one morning I opened the newspaper to read the devastating news: JERRY GIESLER SUFFERS HEART ATTACK.

23

Life Without Rock

"MR. GIESLER is terribly ill," his secretary told me. "His doctors won't allow him to do any work. Under the circumstances, you might be wise to consult another attorney."

I felt so sorry for this wise, compassionate man, with whom I had felt safe and comfortable. I needed to get on with my divorce, and a friend suggested another prominent Los Angeles lawyer whom I'll call Roger Henley. I made an appointment, and I found him in a huge office, his desk on a small platform, spotlights shining down on his head. He seemed large, but when he descended to my level to shake my hand, I discovered he was my height. We chatted for a while, but mostly he wanted to tell me about his brown belt in karate.

Then we got down to business.

"How much do you want?" he asked.

"Whatever is fair," I said.

"How much does he have?"

"I don't really know. I never knew his finances. I couldn't even sign checks until a few months ago. I do know that after I took him to the Morgan Maree office, he had to turn back a big check to Selznick so he could renegotiate with Universal. But I'm sure that has been resolved and he's getting paid again."

Within my heart I believed that Rock would take care of me. After all, we had lived together for almost three years. We had loved each other—I'm certain of that. I think that most women facing divorce believe, at least during the initial stages, that their husbands will take care of them. How naïve. I should have realized that Henry was poisoning Rock's mind against me. Rock was so malleable, so susceptible to influence. He hated to make decisions, so Henry made them for him.

My new attorney reported back to me that the other side wasn't offering much. The alimony would be $250 a week for ten years. I would keep the Sparrow house, for which Rock had paid $32,000, my car, and most of the wedding presents. They wanted me to return the 5 percent interest in Rock's company that he had given me as an anniversary present.

"Don't you dare give that up," Kathy L'Amour advised me.

I refused to part with my percentage, and that proved to be the only wise thing I did in the divorce. A few years later, I asked my attorney, Jim Smith, to inquire about my interest in Rock's company, the 7 Picture Corporation. It turned out that 7 Pictures had moved its assets—which were Rock's services—to a new company, Gibraltar. The move was an obvious ploy to get rid of Henry Ginsburg, who owned 35 percent of 7 Pictures, as well as me and my 5 percent (Rock owned 36 percent and Henry Willson 16 percent). Jim Smith proved that the transfer was invalid. I was awarded $130,000, minus $30,000 for attorney's fees.

The alimony now seems paltry considering Rock's earning power and the harm that he had caused me. But I wasn't thinking in financial terms at the time. I was too emotional, too desperate to close the most painful portion of my life. I agreed to the terms.

When I went to my attorney's office to sign the papers, he wasn't there. Another lawyer presented them to me, and he said, "Mrs. Hudson, what is the matter with you? This is peanuts!" I shrugged and signed.

AUGUST 13, 1958. Santa Monica Superior Court.

I came with my attorney and Pat Devlin, who was going to testify on my behalf. We arrived first and took our places in the courtroom. Soon Rock arrived, flanked by his high-powered lawyer and the ever-present Henry Willson. How appropriate, I thought. Henry was present at the creation of my marriage, and here he is at the dissolution.

Rock wore a dark suit, which contrasted with the paleness of his face. He seemed petrified. Henry looked nervous too. They had good reason to be scared. In the next few minutes I could destroy Rock's multimillion-dollar career with what I knew.

I took the witness stand first. I gave my name, Phyllis Gates Fitzgerald, and the details of our wedding. I told how Rock didn't like to dress up in a coat and tie and so he seldom took me out socially, except for business occasions. How he failed to come home from Italy when I was seriously ill with hepatitis.

"He was terribly moody and wouldn't talk to me for days, sometimes weeks," I testified. "He is never home, and he has hit me twice and he tried to choke me once."

The judge, Edward R. Brand, who had been listening distractedly, suddenly looked stern. He looked at Rock and then at me, as if comparing Rock's six-feet-six frame and my five-feet-six.

Pat came on the witness stand, and the lawyer asked her, "Did you ever see Mr. Hudson strike his wife, Phyllis?"

"Yes," Pat answered. "We were driving back from Laguna one night and he backhanded her across the face for no apparent reason."

Judge Brand's face clouded further. He quickly noted the property settlement and pounded his gavel: "Divorce granted on grounds of mental cruelty."

It was over. Rock didn't look at me, nor did I look at him. He hurried out of the courtroom with his agent and lawyer on either side, protecting their valuable client, it seemed. How relieved they must have felt, as if the world had been lifted from their shoulders. I had the power to destroy Rock but I didn't use it. To have exposed his other life would have been vicious and vindictive. I faced enough trouble rebuilding my life without bearing that guilt.

THE POST-DIVORCE BLUES set in.

On a surface level, my lifestyle had made an abrupt change. No more fancy dresses for premieres and parties. No first-class travel all over the world, staying in luxury hotels. No more limos to take me anywhere, maître d's bowing me to the best table. The party was over.

More importantly, I had lost something of myself. My self-esteem had plummeted. I felt insecure and rejected.

"You did the right thing, Phyllis," Dr. Dubois reassured me. "There wasn't any hope for your marriage. You would have subjugated everything you believed in. You couldn't have won without destroying yourself."

Dr. Dubois continued: "The reason you became so sick, Phyllis, is because you had regressed in order to please Rock. You had become childlike, just like him. Remember how you used to like tiny dolls and animals when you were a young girl. You were becoming like that again, taking delight in little things. You adored little Demi. That's why I insisted that you get a big dog after you lost Demi. You are an adult, Phyllis. You could not have been happy living in Rock's childish world."

She was right. Perhaps I could have stayed married to Rock, having the luxuries of a movie star's life without his love. Many women have remained in unhappy marriages because they don't want to face financial insecurity. I'm sure Henry would have preferred for me to remain Mrs. Rock Hudson, in name only, so Rock's reputation would not be endangered. Famous homosexuals have been known to maintain wives as cover-ups.

Once a friend asked me how I could give up the fame and money of being Rock Hudson's wife. "For self-preservation," I replied. I could tell by the look on his face he didn't understand. I didn't explain.

The blues I felt after the divorce were accompanied by a physical malaise. In November I consulted Dr. Brandsma, and after a number of tests, he sent me to St. John's Hospital for gall bladder surgery. My visit to the hospital was different this time. When I had hepatitis, I was flooded with bouquets and cards. Now I received a few flowers from close friends. But they meant more to me than all of the studio gifts.

I came home after a week in the hospital, and I recovered quickly. When the doctor and hospital bills started coming in, I called the Morgan Maree office to ask about insurance. "Oh, your policy has been canceled," I was told. Wonderful! I had enormous bills for my operation and no way to pay them. So I sold some of my jewelry.

Soon it was Christmas. Sue and Alan Ladd invited me to the Christmas Eve buffet dinner they gave every year. Outside their door was a life-size mechanical Santa Claus who nodded to all the guests. The house was ablaze with lights and color, with a Christmas tree that reached to the high ceiling. The den was filled with round tables with red tablecloths and white chairs. On the buffet table, silver serving dishes were laden with steaming, festive food. Everyone was dressed to the nines, and the conversation was bright and witty.

I forgot about the surgery. I decided that night that I was going to try to live again. I had to get over my sorrow and pain, and no one else could help me. I had to do it by myself.

Epilogue

BACK TO SCHOOL.

Dr. Dubois had continued urging me to go to college. She wanted me to study psychology because she felt I had good instincts about people and cared about them. "That is the sign of a good psychologist," she said. "You don't know how much you understand, and the wonderful part is you're not judgmental. A psychologist cannot be judgmental. People who strive for perfection in themselves are usually the people who judge. They want their friends to be as perfect as they think they are. Nobody should strive for perfection. Number one, it is impossible. Secondly, who would want it?"

Another mentor was Dr. Fred Mayer. He was a professor of philosophy at the University of Redlands, and I had met him through Kathy and Lou L'Amour. I often had dinner with Dr. Mayer, and the talk centered around people, motivations, and values. He was a humanitarian, devoted to helping people. "You must go to college, Phyllis," he urged me.

After I took a vacation to Hawaii, Dr. Mayer helped me register at Redlands. At age thirty-three I was going to college!

Every Monday morning I drove the sixty miles to Redlands and left Gretchen at the apartment I had rented. During the week I attended classes, studied, and took part in the intellectual ferment of a university campus. Because I had no classes on Friday, I returned to Los Angeles on Thursday afternoon. Dr. Dubois was right: it was exactly what I needed. I forgot about Rock Hudson, the divorce, and Hollywood. I came alive.

I earned good grades in my first semester at Redlands, but the weekly drive and maintaining two residences proved impractical. I decided to enroll at the University of Southern California. First I needed to take some math and language courses at UCLA Extension. On my first day in French class, a young man walked over and said, "You're the prettiest girl here. Would you like a cup of coffee?"

I looked up startled. Here was this California type—muscular build, blond crew cut, perfect smile, six feet two—giving me the come-on. I was too startled to brush him off.

Over coffee in the co-op we learned about each other. His name was Greg, and he was a law student at USC, taking a French course at UCLA for extra credit.

"I'm hoping to get into USC next spring," I announced.

"Great!" he said. "We can have lunch together."

I wanted to take a music appreciation course that summer, and so did he. So we both enrolled at UCLA Extension, and we spent hours listening to Bach, Liszt, Chopin, and Haydn. Greg also took me to some of his favorite bars, small places where we drank beer and listened to banjo music. We always ended up at my house where we studied —and made love.

Sometimes I said to myself, "Phyllis, what *are* you doing? This man is ten years younger than you are. You know there's no future in this affair."

I knew that, but I didn't care. I also knew that Greg stimulated my mind as well as my libido, that we made each other laugh, that he made me feel wanted and useful. That was enough for the moment. Dr. Mayer had converted me into a true pragmatist.

In the fall, Greg returned to his law studies at USC and I continued courses I needed for the entrance exam there. We continued seeing each other many evenings, and we spent weekends in Palm Springs.

I passed the USC entrance exam, and carried a heavy course load my first semester. But I managed. In the summer I returned to UCLA for courses in abnormal psychology, anatomy, and literature. Then back to USC in the fall.

After two years, Greg left for San Francisco to continue his law studies at the Hastings campus of the University of California. We parted in the best Cole Porter manner, without rancor, without regret. It was great fun, but it was just one of those things.

Over the years there have been other men in my life. I almost married one of them. But I could never bring myself to fall in love again. To me, love was associated with pain.

After Greg left, I had companions to occupy me. Camus. Stendhal. Gide. Eliot. Chekov. Dostoevski. As well as Michelangelo, Renoir, and Van Gogh. I took many art classes, working in oils and in watercolor combined with ink, my particular favorite. I attended USC for three years. Together with Redlands and UCLA, I accumulated one hundred units.

Somewhere in all my reading, I learned that the greatest thing for self-development is to sell all your worldly goods and move to a country where you don't know the language.

It seemed like a good idea for me. It had become difficult for me to maintain the Sparrow house. Fires had swept the hillsides, and my insurance had tripled. The property tax was rising. I had no income except the $250 weekly alimony. To raise money, I sold my wedding ring and the gold cocktail purse Rock had brought me from Italy. Still, I was falling behind.

I decided it was time to move on. My studies had instilled a desire to learn about other cultures. I put the Sparrow house on the market, and it sold almost immediately for $38,000, a sure sign that it was priced too low. I didn't care.

Before leaving, I had one piece of unfinished business.

I had been using the name of Phyllis Hudson (even though it was legally Fitzgerald). One day a student at USC asked me, "Are you the Phyllis Hudson who used to be married to Rock Hudson?"

"No," I lied.

"Funny, you sure do look like her."

I never talked to anyone about Rock, nor did I admit to new friends that I had been married to him. When my old friends tried to tell me the latest gossip about Rock, I told them, "Thanks, but I don't want to hear it." I needed to keep my distance from all the memories.

On July 14, 1964, Jim Smith and I went to court in Santa Monica. It was the same courthouse where my divorce had been granted, and I felt a twinge of pain as I climbed the steps.

The judge questioned me about my birthplace, my family, the circumstances of my marriage. Then he asked, "Why do you want your maiden name back?"

"Because the name of Hudson brings back memories of unhappiness," I answered.

"Name change granted."

Again I was Phyllis Gates. Myself. Alone and independent. I felt renewed, revitalized, ready for a new adventure.

PARIS WAS DIFFERENT this time. No palatial suite at the Plaza Athénée, no limousine to take me anywhere I wanted. My hotel was on the Left Bank, directly across from the Louvre. My French was miserable, so I enrolled in a language class at the Alliance Français. I wanted to communicate with the French people. Fortunately, friends had given me names of Parisians who proved very hospitable. I ate lunch and dinner at a small bistro near my hotel, and that became a second home.

I spent an eventful year in Europe, studying with a French artist, visiting Hjördis and David Niven in Switzerland, touring Normandy with friends, visiting Madrid and Toledo, spending a sunny month in St. Tropez.

No one knew about my marriage to Rock Hudson. Then French television offered a week of his movies, and the television guide carried a photograph of Rock and me. My cover was blown.

"Is it true that you were married to Rock Hudson?" my friend Colette asked.

"Yes," I admitted.

"Oh," she replied, and nothing more was said. My friends realized that I didn't want to talk about my marriage, and they never mentioned it.

By September 1965 I felt it was time to go home. I had been on a journey to find myself, and I believed that I had succeeded. Mainly I needed to rid myself of false values. All that glamour. Unquestionably, it was intoxicating. But I realized that, like all intoxicants, it could be destructive.

BACK IN LOS ANGELES, I rented a small apartment and renewed my friendships, mostly with people outside the movie business. I had become fascinated with antiques in Europe, and for a time I worked in a furniture shop. Pat Devlin married Murray Swafford in November 1966, and I fulfilled the second half of our vow to stand up at each other's wedding. Pat and Murray ran a golfing-tour company, and for a time I worked for them, taking tours to far-off resorts.

One day before Christmas, in 1968, my sister Verna telephoned me from Minnesota with the news that my father had been taken to a hospital in Minneapolis. It was cancer, inoperable.

I flew to Minneapolis to be with my mother during the long hours of waiting at the hospital. The doctors decided he could go home to the Montevideo hospital. There was no hope for recovery, but he would receive adequate care, and he would be among his family and friends.

I returned to Montevideo in the summer and fall of 1969, and I talked on the telephone with Mom almost every day. In the spring Dad's condition worsened. By this time the trips home and the telephone bills had depleted my savings. I was desperate. I would never forgive myself if I didn't see Dad again before he died. I also knew that I would have to make another trip to Montevideo for the funeral.

How desperate was I? Enough to ask Rock for a loan.

I wrote to him, care of the Morgan Maree office, telling him of my father's illness and my lack of cash. Would he please lend me two hundred dollars, which I would pay back as soon as I was able?

Rock, who was then earning a half million dollars per film, didn't reply. After two weeks of waiting, I telephoned a friend in Sausalito, Floyd Nelson, a United Airlines captain. He wired me the money immediately.

Dad died July 16, 1970.

WHILE I WAS IN NEW YORK in 1971, a friend offered me a job in the design business. I accepted, and I stayed in New York for five years until the cold weather finally got to my weak leg. I decided to move to Palm Springs. I bought a house and started working for a decorator.

My job required many trips to Los Angeles. I needed a place to stay overnight, also a refuge from the fierce desert summers. I called a real estate agent and told her my needs. "Too bad you missed a house up in the bird streets. It's a probate sale."

"Where in the bird streets, Mildred?" I asked. "I used to live up there."

When she told me the address, I nearly dropped the phone. "My God, that's my old house!" I said.

She explained that the probate executor had already accepted a bid from a couple who wanted to use the house while they built one of their own. "I'd like to see it, anyway," I said.

I could hardly recognize the place. The owner had died, and his stepson had occupied it with three musicians. Beer bottles were everywhere. The beautiful pegged-wood floor was obscured by crushed pretzels and debris. A set of drums was in the living room. Each bedroom had mattresses on the floor. The hillside and trees were completely overgrown.

It was the only house I could afford. The couple's deal fell through, and I went to probate court to bid for the house. Unfortunately, another buyer wanted the house, and the bidding rose to $296,000 before I won. This was the same place I had sold for $38,000 twenty years before.

The barn-red color was changed to light beige with white windowsills. The floors were sanded and refinished— this time I had the sense not to carpet them. The hillside was trimmed, the trees pruned, and I planted lots of flowers.

And what did I feel, returning to the house where I had known great happiness—and great sorrow?

Nothing. Not at first. The house was so different, the events so long ago—and pushed into the depths of my memory out of need to survive—that I felt nothing. The shock was still to come.

I SAW HENRY WILLSON one more time after our encounter in the divorce court. A few years later, I was dining in a Hollywood restaurant with a friend. Out of the corner of my eye I noticed someone take a chair opposite me at our table. I knew immediately who it was. But I didn't look at him. I continued conversing with my date, totally ignoring the intruder. After a few minutes, he left the table.

I have learned of Henry's later history by talking to some of his former clients. They told me that Henry remained Rock's agent for a few years after our divorce, then Rock dropped him. It was a devastating blow to Henry, and his agency went downhill thereafter. In 1967, he moved with his remaining clients to a larger agency, but it became obvious he had lost his touch. Pretty boys with trick names were no longer in vogue.

By the early 1970s, Henry was on the skids. He became an alcoholic, cadging drinks from friends until they learned to avoid him. At one point he tried to kill himself, and he was committed to a psychiatric ward. Henry spent his last days at the Motion Picture and Television Country House in Woodland Hills. A friend who visited him said all Henry talked about was the ingratitude of his former clients, especially Rock.

Henry died on November 2, 1978, at the age of sixty-seven. Only a few of his old clients—Rory Calhoun, Chad Everett, Tom Irish, a few others—attended the funeral. The burial place was a dismal spot next to the freeway. The mourners chipped in to buy Henry a better plot in Forest Lawn. "He deserves to go out with a little class," one of them said.

AFTER ROCK DIED, George Nader and Mark Miller called me. It was a surprise, since I hadn't talked to either of them in thirty years. "We would like you to come to Rock's memorial service at the house," Mark said.

"No, I couldn't do that," I said. It would have been hypocritical for me to appear at a memorial for the man I hadn't seen since we parted in the divorce court in 1958.

George called me again, this time to urge me to cooperate with the writer he and Mark had chosen to write Rock's "autobiography." When I declined, he urged me, saying: "Just six months before he died, Rock said he had loved only two people in his life. One of them was you. I really believe, Phyllis, that the only time I knew Rock to be really happy was when he was married to you."

Still I resisted, but that didn't stop the author from calling me with persistent questions.

When I decided to write this book, my friends rallied to my help. Pat Devlin Swafford, my friend from my first day at the Willson Agency to the present time, was the first to volunteer. We talked for hours, trying to dredge up long-forgotten memories. "I couldn't believe it when I learned that Rock was bisexual," Pat said. "I never would have thought it."

Dr. Maynard Brandsma, who has studied the problem of AIDS, came up from his home in Mission Viejo to assist me with his wisdom and recollections. He had been Henry Willson's physician, and Henry sent many of his clients, including Rock, to Dr. Brandsma. With his keen eye, Maynard could easily detect which of his patients were homosexual.

"I knew about Rock," he told me. "I debated with myself whether I should warn you. I could see what you were getting into. I had seen it happen before, with both male and female, and it was always very tragic and sad. But if you tell them beforehand, they just don't believe you. They are so much in love that they think you're a bastard and it would be a good thing for you to be shot." I remembered that after my premarital exam, Dr. Brandsma and his nurse had been locked in a serious conversation. They had been discussing whether or not he should tell me about Rock. He decided against it, reasoning, probably correctly, that I wouldn't believe him.

Jim Smith, my attorney and a man who has helped me in many matters, told me: "Phyllis, you were Rock's only friend. You did everything for him. You must have saved him hundreds of thousands of dollars by getting him out of Henry Willson's clutches and into the Maree office."

There were others who helped me remember the events of thirty years ago: Ray Stricklyn, John Carlyle, John Smith, Tom Irish, Ben Pearson.

Bit by bit, I have tried to piece together the enigma that was Rock Hudson. Dr. Dubois had told me that when she gave the psychological tests to Rock, he showed the emotional development of a ten-year-old. Indeed, he was childlike in both ways. The good: ingratiating personality; delight in gifts and small pleasures; talent for playacting. The bad: fierce, uncontrollable temper; capacity to lie to himself and others; living for the present. Rock never talked about his past, nor was he concerned about the future. Everything was here and now, regardless of the consequences. Because of this heedlessness, he hurt other people, including me, and, eventually, himself.

To me, Rock seemed like the Laurence Harvey character in *Room at the Top*, using people as stepping-stones until he himself was totally corrupted, an empty human being incapable of feelings. Or, as Albert Camus wrote in *The Fall*:

Thus I progressed on the surface of life, in the realm of words, as it were, never in reality. All those books barely read, those friends barely loved, those cities barely visited, those women barely possessed.

I have a friend who believes in psychic reality. She says I was destined to return to this house I shared with Rock Hudson. Thus I could write the book and free myself forever of the demons. Now, she says, having written it, I should move out. Perhaps she is right.